REA's
Quick & Easy Guide to
Writing Your
A+ Term Paper

Staff of Research & Education Association
Dr. M. Fogiel, Director

ST. EDMUND'S ACADEMY
5705 DARLINGTON ROAD
PITTSBURGH, PA 15217

Research & Education Association

61 Ethel Road West, Piscataway, New Jersey 08854

REA's Quick & Easy Guide to
WRITING YOUR A+ TERM PAPER

1999 PRINTING

Printed in the United States of America

Library of Congress Catalog Card Number 97-68603

International Standard Book Number 0-87891-785-3

 **Research & Education Association**
61 Ethel Road West
Piscataway, New Jersey 08854

sample title page

Title of Paper

Your Name

Name of Course

Instructor's Name

Date

TABLE OF CONTENTS

How to Use this Book vii

Sample Outline ix

Margin Specification Model xi

Writing Your A+ Term Paper 1

    I.   Choosing the Topic 3

        Topics, Purposes, and Points 4

    II. Gathering Material 6

        An Overview of the Steps and Sources 7

        General Reference Material 10

        Card and Computer Catalogs 11

        Indexes for Periodicals and Other Materials 14

        Bibliography Cards 18

        Evaluating Sources 22

        Notecards 23

   III. Composing the Paper 24

        The Outline and Organizing the Main Points 24

        Parts of the Term Paper 25

        Writing the Rough Draft 26

        Revising, Editing, and Proofreading 27

   IV. Preparing Your Paper for Presentation 28

        The Paper, Margins, Typing, and Binding 28

        The Title Page 30

        The Outline 31

        Footnotes 32

        Quotations and Appendices 38

        Bibliography 40

        The Final Check 40

Helpful Hints on Grammar and Writing 43

   I. Guidelines for Punctuation Marks 45

      End Punctuation Marks 45

      Internal Punctuation Marks 50

   II. Common Sentence Errors 75

      Dangling Modifiers 75

      Misplaced Modifiers 75

      Lack of Parallel Structure 77

      Sentence Fragments 79

      Run-On Sentences 80

      Comma Splices 81

      Short, Choppy Sentences—Sentence Variation 81

      Wordiness 82

      Rambling Sentences 83

   III. Words Commonly Confused and Misused 84

Sample Appendix 95

Sample Bibliography 97

HOW TO USE THIS HANDBOOK

Its Uses:

This handbook has been written to be used (1) as an overview of the steps and skills needed to write a successful term paper, (2) as a specific guide to each step of the organizing, researching, composing, and editing processes, and (3) as a source for examples and rules of correct usage and writing structure.

To use the information presented in this handbook to your best advantage, you should first read the entire book to become familiar with what goes into writing a term paper. Then, as you begin the process of writing your term paper, use this book to guide you through the specific steps as you complete them. During the composing, editing, and revising steps you should reference the sections on grammar and correct sentence structure whenever you have a question about a sentence or word.

The Sections:

To enhance your understanding of the creation of a term paper, this guide to writing a term paper has been organized into four main sections: Choosing the Topic, Gathering Material, Composing the Paper, and Preparing Your Paper for Presentation. Each section is placed in the chronological order in which you will encounter it as you write your term paper. As you complete each section, it would help you best to review the material in the section and double-check that you have completed all of the steps and understand all of the information presented. A fifth section, Helpful Hints on Grammar and Writing, has been included as a reference for students encountering difficulties during the composing, editing, and revising stages of writing a term paper.

The Examples:

You should notice that examples of term paper pages are given throughout this handbook to visually aid you in preparing your term paper. There are examples of a title page, outline, appendix, and bibliography. You should use these examples as models when creating your term paper. Your finished title page, outline, appendices, and bibliography should look very similar to examples provided in this handbook.

Throughout the text you will also notice examples of footnotes and bibliography formats. Once again, these examples have been provided to give you a visual reference of what the elements of your term paper will look like.

Finally, we have included examples of reference indexes and menu screens from a computerized library catalog. You should use these examples to familiarize yourself with the organization and wording of these sources before going to the library. If you know what to expect before you go to the library then you will be able to find what you are looking for faster. In addition, you'll be able to find more sources and feel more confident that you have found all of the available information on your topic.

Sample Outline of a
Term Paper

I. Choosing the Topic
    A. Limiting the Subject
    B. Availability of Materials
    C. Interest in the Subject
    D. Topics, Purposes, and Points

II. Gathering Material
    A. An Overview of the Steps and Sources
    B. General Reference Material
    C. Card and Computer Catalogs
    D. Indexes for Periodicals and Other Materials
    E. Bibliography Cards
        1. one-author books
        2. two-author books
        3. multiple-author books
        4. one-editor books
        5. one-translator books
        6. compilation books or anthologies
        7. periodicals
        8. encyclopedia articles
    F. Evaluating Sources
    G. Notecards

III. Composing the Paper
    A. The Outline and Organizing the Main Points
    B. Parts of the Term Paper
    C. Writing the Rough Draft
    D. Revising, Editing, and Proofreading

IV. Preparing Your Paper for Presentation
    A. The Paper, Margins, Typing, and Binding
    B. The Title Page
    C. The Outline
    D. Footnotes
        1. one-author books
        2. two-author and multiple-author books
        3. one-editor and one-translator books
        4. compilation books and anthologies
        5. periodicals and encyclopedia articles
        6. special citations
        7. repeat footnotes
    E. Quotations and Appendices
    F. Bibliography
    G. The Final Check

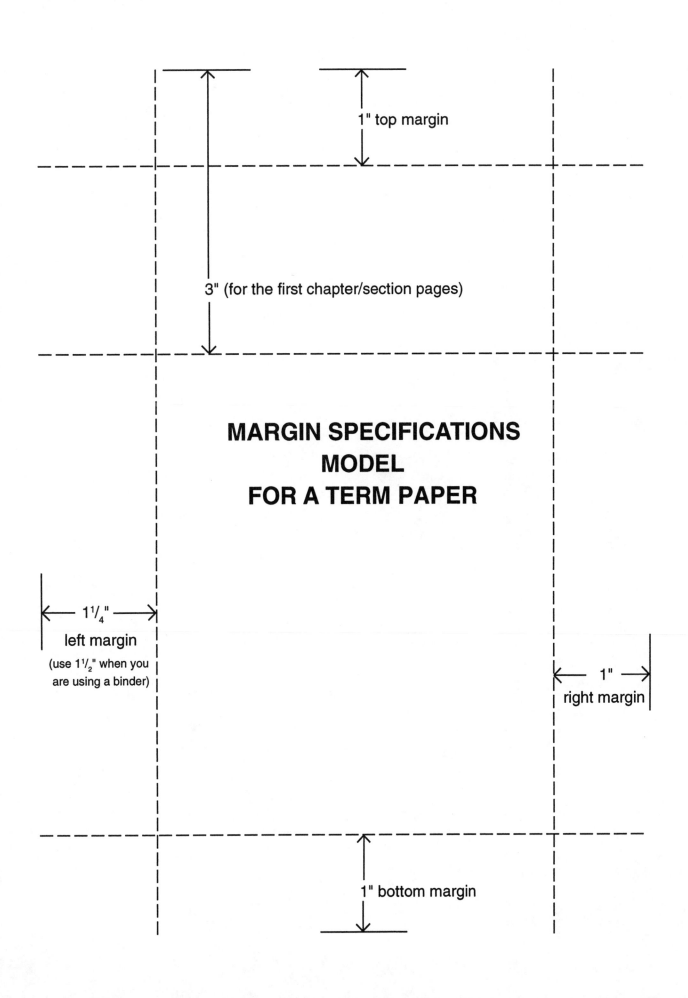

1" top margin

3" (for the first chapter/section pages)

**MARGIN SPECIFICATIONS
MODEL
FOR A TERM PAPER**

← 1¹⁄₄" →
left margin
(use 1¹⁄₂" when you
are using a binder)

← 1" →
right margin

1" bottom margin

WRITING YOUR A+ TERM PAPER

I. Choosing the Topic

Many things should influence the choice of a topic for your term paper. When a teacher assigns a term paper, certain restrictions are often placed on the students. If the length of the paper is established, this should have a direct bearing on the topic. For example, can the topic "Causes of World War II" be adequately treated in a three-page paper? A writer must learn to limit his or her subject. Also, does the topic lend itself to the assignment? Would such a theme as the influence of the Beatles on the 60s generation be an appropriate topic for a term paper? You must answer these questions before any writing is done. But perhaps the most important question in the choice of a topic is interest. If a writer knows little about a topic he or she must ask one basic question: "Do I have enough curiosity to investigate this topic further?" Nothing is more tedious than writing about something which is of no interest. This boredom is often expressed in the style of the writing and the reader will also suffer.

When deciding on an interesting topic to write on, you must take into account another factor: availability of materials. A topic can be the most interesting subject in the world, but if you only have one 20-page book to use as a source for a 1,000-word term paper, then that topic cannot be used. You must have access to useful books, reference books, and periodicals from which to collect information for the term paper. When you are about to make a decision on a topic, the amount of material available—meaning in nearby libraries—is a very important factor. Some preliminary library research and a knowledge of the topic can help in deciding whether there is sufficient material available to use a particular topic.

Many teachers will assign topics to write about; others will allow you to choose their own topics. A topic is any subject of study, inquiry, or discussion that is addressed for the sake of an audience. A topic, however, is not a purpose or main point. Remember that a topic is the subject about which the author writes. Books, cars, people, sports, rainbows, fish, potato chips—anything can be a topic of inquiry, study, or discussion. The first step is to choose one and begin to focus on writing about it.

Some topics are too broad to deal with in a short 500-word paper so the teacher may ask that the topic be narrowed. Narrowing a topic means limiting it and becoming more specific about what is to be discussed in the paper, making it a manageable length and scope.

Topics, Purposes, and Points

Term papers would be pointless without an audience. Why write a term paper if no one wants to read it? Why add evidence, organize your ideas, or correct bad grammar? The reason to do any of these things is because someone out there needs to understand what you mean or say.

What does the audience need to know in order to believe you or to come over to your position? Imagine someone you know listening to you declare your position or opinion and then saying, "Oh, yeah? Prove it!" This is your audience—write to them. Ask yourself the following questions so that you will not be confronted with a person who says, "Prove it!"

- What evidence do I need to prove my idea to this skeptic?
- What would she or he disagree with me about?
- What does he or she share with me as common knowledge?
- What do I need to tell the reader?

Once a topic has been chosen, the purpose of the paper must be defined. Usually papers are written to explain, persuade, tell a story, or describe some object, experience, or theory.

If surfing is the topic of a paper, for example, then you might explain what surfing is or how it is done. Likewise, you could try to persuade the reader to surf or not to surf. A story could be told of some famous or exceptional surfer, or else of an outstanding incident in your own surfing experience. A description of the experience of surfing is another possibility.

After defining the purpose of the paper, the point of the paper must be established. What end are you trying to achieve? Although the point might be obvious, it is still a good idea to summarize it in one sentence.

If the topic is fishing, for example, and the purpose is to explain what fishing is and how it is done, a point must now be established. Certainly, it is not just to write a collection of facts about fishing. This would be boring even to a fisherman. You should return to your interest in the topic. If you have knowledge about the subject, for example, there must also be some general feelings on the subject. A conclusion is drawn or an observation made which links all the facts in the paper together. If you enjoy fishing, this could become the point of the paper.

Some examples of topics, purposes, and points are given below.

Topic:	Sewing
Purpose:	To describe how it felt to sew my sister's wedding dress
Point:	Being able to sew made it possible for me to have an exciting experience.

Topic:	Submarines
Purpose:	To explain how submarines work
Point:	Submarines work on very simple principles.

Topic:	Summer camp
Purpose:	To tell the story of an awful experience at summer camp
Point:	Summer camp is not always fun.

You should be in no rush to get to the typewriter. Inspiration alone is rarely the source of a good paper. If writing is the craft of expressing ideas, then you must have clear ideas to begin with. Take time to think and organize before going into a frenzy of writing.

II. Gathering Material

Writing a term paper is a long-term project; consequently, time must be scheduled during a term so that the completed paper can be delivered on time. Since the term paper must go through the same stages as any essay, use the stages of the writing process to plan time. Whatever time you have, a paper should be scheduled in such a manner that it can be completed by your teacher's deadline.

Your term paper is basically another paper that must be written using the writing process. During the prewriting stage, use the time you have to gather research at the library. Do not hesitate to seek the help of a research librarian in the library at your high school or college. Research librarians can point out where to find the information sources the writer needs.

An Overview of the Steps and Sources

Basically, you may find research material in either a card catalog or a computer catalog. Most libraries now have computer catalogs, so it is helpful to become computer literate to use them effectively. Sources that should be sought out in the library include, of course, books relevant to the topic that can be found in the Library of Congress subject headings or, in some libraries, in the Dewey Decimal System. These are the systems used to catalog information in most libraries. You must learn to use the systems to find what you need.

```
  261 Alexander Library       --IRIS Library System - All * Choose
  Search
What type of search do you wish to do?
    1. TIL - Title, journal title, series title, etc.
    2. AUT - Author, illustrator, editor, organization, etc.
    3. SUB - Subject heading assigned by library.
    4. NUM - Call number, ISBN, ISSN, etc.
    5. BOL - Boolean/Keyword search on title, author, and
             subject.
    6. LIM - Limit your search to a portion of the catalogue.


Enter number or code, then press enter <CR>; to exit type END:
```

Figure 1: An example of a main menu from a computer catalog.

In addition to books, you may use periodicals and journals that are relevant to the topic. The Reader's Guide to Periodical Literature and New York Times Index are the two best sources for this information. Indexes for special disciplines such as psychology or medicine are available. Finally, various abstracting services are available to provide summaries of important recent articles and books relevant to a project.

After having discovered how to use these resources, you should develop a working bibliography, that is, a list on index cards of all the sources that might be used in the paper. You must be sure to include all the bibliographic information on one side of the cards (including author, title, publisher, city of publication, year of publication, and any other identifying information necessary). Put important notes on the other side of the cards, such as the author's thesis or main supporting evidence. You should do this in the beginning; so these notes will be available when you are writing the formal bibliography at the end.

```
Bradley, Walter L. et al. The Mystery of Life's Origin.
    New York: The Philosophical Library, 1984.
```

Figure 2: Side One, sample card for working bibliography.

```
┌─────────────────────────────────────────────────────────┐
│                                                           │
│   Thesis:              The beginning of life on earth     │
│                        can be re-created in the           │
│                        laboratory by copying the          │
│                        environment of that time in the    │
│                        history of the Earth.              │
│                                                           │
│                                                           │
│   Of Importance:       Prehistoric Soup; Thermodynamics   │
│                        of life and living systems; and    │
│                        reassessing Earth's early          │
│                        atmosphere.                        │
│                                                           │
│                                                           │
│                                                           │
└─────────────────────────────────────────────────────────┘
```

Figure 3: Side Two, sample card for working bibliography.

A term paper is a formal argument that will be judged on its thoroughness, its reasoning, and the supporting evidence for that reasoning. The research you conduct for your paper will provide the thoroughness and supporting evidence. You will find that once you have informed yourself about a topic, opinions and reasoning will follow. Working from this realization, a calculated, organized approach to your research cannot help but strengthen your term paper.

In researching sources for your term paper, bibliography cards will prove to be an invaluable tool for keeping track of your findings. Not only do they simplify the writing of the paper's final bibliography (when time can be precious), the cards are a handy form in which to access your working list of sources. With one item per card, you will later have multiple options for organizing your materials—chronologically, by form (books, periodicals, or other), or by the planned sequence of your paper.

General Reference Material

Often the simplest way to begin your research is to read about your subject in a general encyclopedia. This will introduce you to the areas you need to re-search, and give you a basis for a list of subjects and names to work from when you get to the card catalog. For the beginning, however, continue working in the reference section so that you can expand and refine your subject list. You will want to consult the "standard" initial sources first. From the general encyclope-dias, your next step may vary with your topic. If the subject of your paper is a specific person, consult the Who's Who texts, which range from the general to the specific. Many scientific subjects are covered individually in specialized encyclopedias and dictionaries. This is also true for some humanities and social science subjects. These specialized reference books will turn up when you go to the card catalog, so do not worry if you do not see one on your topic right away. They are also accessible from other reference books as you will see.

The following list gives a selection of common useful reference texts. The first two sections name the texts you should consult at this initial stage of your research, and the second two sections list others for more advanced research, which will be discussed later:

Encyclopedia Britannica

Encyclopedia Americana

The Columbia Encyclopedia

The World Almanac

Who's Who, Who's Who in American Women, Who's Who in Religion,

Who Was Who in American Politics, etc.

Biography Index

Dictionary of American Biography

McGraw-Hill Encyclopedia of Science and Technology

Dictionary of Literary Terms

Oxford English Dictionary

Reader's Guide to Periodical Literature

The New York Times Index

Book Review Digest

Guide to Reference Books

First Step: The Master Index to Subject Encyclopedias

Register of Indexes

Books in Print

Facts on File

Arts and Humanities Citation Index

Science Citation Index

Social Sciences Citation Index

Card and Computer Catalogs

By now you know what key terms and names are relevant to your paper topic, and you can bring that knowledge to bear at the library's catalogs. Today, even local township libraries have computerized catalogs that allow you to enter a key word and get a list of related texts. As convenient as this seems, be sure to address the same subject with as many synonyms as you can think of, because the program's cross-referencing may not always be ideal. You should also supplement the computer's output by checking the card catalog. Sometimes certain references fall through the cracks between supposedly redundant cata-logs. For the same reason, technology-haters should not forego consulting the computer catalog. Philosophies and therefore cataloguing priorities change from library to library.

```
261 Alexander Library      --IRIS Library System - All * Choose
Search

   For people, enter last name first.

        EX:  Bronte, Emily

        EX:  Mondrian, Piet

For other authors, use normal word order.

        EX:  National Research Council

        EX:  Rutgers University


   Enter Author:    Then press SEND
```

Figure 4: An example of the menu for a computer catalog search by author.

```
261 Alexander Library      --IRIS Library System - All * Choose
Search

         Start at the beginning of the title and enter as many
      words of the title as you know below.

         EX:  Wuthering Heights

         EX:  How to Succeed in Business Without


   Enter title:         Then press SEND
```

Figure 5: An example of the menu for a computer catalog search by title.

```
261 Alexander Library      --IRIS Library System - All * Choose
Search

      Start at the beginning of the Library of Congress sub-
      ject heading and enter as many words of the subject
      heading as you know below. Choose the most specific
      subject heading you can.

            EX:  molecular biology (NOT biology)

            EX:  feminism and literature (NOT literature)


   Enter subject:    Then press SEND
```

Figure 6: An example of the menu for a computer catalog search by subject.

Another method of double checking the cross-referencing of a catalog is to use all three of its bases for catalog entry. Each book is entered under its title, its author, and its subject. If a subject search produces a book that sounds like it will be useful in your term paper, look up the author to inspect his or her other works. This practice eliminates the chance of many cross-referencing omissions. Also, a title search should show you all editions of the text, allowing you to verify that you will be using the most recent edition. It is not unusual for prefaces to change with subsequent editions, so do not automatically discount earlier editions—you may find useful quotes in the earlier prefaces.

Remember that the library's catalog only lists the information available in that particular library or library network. As you find useful texts and articles, consult their bibliographies for additional sources. You may find these additional texts at other libraries, be able to borrow them from an instructor, or purchase them. The main point is that these additional sources are easier to find when you know exactly what to ask for.

Indexes for Periodicals and Other Materials

The usefulness of periodicals varies widely from topic to topic, but they should always be consulted. You would be amazed to learn how specific and bizarre some magazine titles are. Note that you will not find periodicals listed in the card catalog. The ultimate authority on periodicals is The Reader's Guide to Periodical Literature, a series of hard-cover volumes, usually green or brown, spanning the past several decades. Each volume covers a year, except the most recent soft-cover volumes, which cover quarters of the current year, and older volumes, which may cover spans of years. Unfortunately, you must repeat your topic scan from volume to volume, but the Reader's Guide is very precise and as you become familiar with its format you will find your information more quickly. Because it is a comprehensive index, the Reader's Guide will list magazines that your library does not have, but you should still record these in your notes. Different libraries have different periodical banks, and later research may compel you to expand your search to other nearby libraries.

SURFACES
     See also
    Interfaces
    Thin films
             Areas and volumes
    The crystalline face of soap films [work of Jean E. Taylor]
        I. Peterson. il *Science News* 134:135 Ag 27 '88
    Geometry for segragating polymers [copolymers; work of Edwin
        L. Thomas and David Hoffman] I. Peterson. il *Science
        News* 134:151 S 3 '88
SURFACTANTS *See* Surface active substances
SURFING
     See also
    Boardsailing
    Bodyboarding
    Ice surfing
    Davey's little surfer girl [A. Johnson] J. Lieber. il pors *Sports
        Illustrated* 69:48+ Jl 25 '88
    In your face, Spuds Mackenzie! Rocky, the beach-blanket
        bowwow, hangs twenty with ease [surfing dog] il *People
        Weekly* 30:66 O 17 '88
    The mechanics of waves–and the art of surfing. R. Woikome
        il *Oceans* 21:36-41 My/Je '88
    Of surf and science [surfing stellar sea lions off coast of
        Vancouver Island] W.M. Roberts. il *Sea Frontiers* 34:48
        N/D '88
    Surf report: tune into the wavelength. il *'Teen* 32:26 Je
        '88
             Equipment
     See also
    Quicksilver, Inc.
             Photographs and photography
    Super surf shooters. P. Skinner. il *Peterson's Photographer
        Magazine* 17:16-20+ Ag '88
SURGEON-GENERAL'S OFFICE (U.S.) *See* United States
    Surgeon General's Office
SURGEONS
     See also
     Kinal, Murl E.
    The best way to find a plastic surgeon. R. Sandroff. il *Working
        Woman* 13:121-2 My '88
    How to check out a surgeon. L. Kleinmann. *Health (New
        York, N.Y.)* 20:8 Ag '88
    Looking for "Doctor Right" [plastic surgeon] J. Schmid. *Vogue*
        178:206+ Ja '88
             Sports
    The whole athlete [plastic surgeon J. Emery] J. Popper. il
        Esquire 109:71-2 Mr '88
SURGEONS AS AUTHORS
    This pen and the scalpel. R. Selzer. il por *The New York
        Times Magazine* p30-1 Ag 21 '88
SURGERY

Figure 7: Example of a listing from The Reader's Guide to Periodical Literature.

For information that would have been "news" at some point, consult The New York Times Index. These volumes, usually red, are organized much like The Reader's Guide to Periodical Literature. Most libraries have the past several decades of The New York Times on microfiche, so these articles will almost always be available. The Sunday New York Times has a magazine section that contains a reputable book review column. These reviews are listed in the Book Review Digest, a separate index. The column's coverage is not limited to bestsellers and novels, and often includes scholarly texts and reference books. Therefore, any subject is worth looking for in the Book Review Digest. Again, those reviews will most often be found on microfiche within that Sunday's The New York Times.

---

damages; drawing (S), D 25, III, 7:2
SULLIVAN, CHRIS. See also
Football, D 28
SUMITOMO METAL INDUSTRIES LTD. See also
Steel and Iron, D 20
SUMMERS, EDWARD L. See also
Murders and Attempted Murders, D 16, 17
SUN, See also
Space, D 20
SUNNI, MUSLIMS. See also
Robberies and Thefts, D 17
SUPERSTITIONS. See also
Astrology
SUPOVE, KATHLEEN. See also
Music, D21
SUPREME COURT (US). See also
Insurance, D 28
  Op-Ed article by Frank Rich says David Brock of The American Spectator proves that tabloid journalism can be practiced in footnoted articles in seemingly sober journals; says his latest victims are Jane Mayer and Jill Abramson, whose new book essentially corroborates Anita Hill's testimony against Supreme Court Justice Clarence Thomas; says Brock, in reviewing book, deliberately falsifies its contents and has tried to bully source in book to get her to sign statement denying her own contribution to book; says his actions threaten reporter's traditional calling of objectively seeking and writing the truth (M), D 29 A, 21:1

```
SUPREME COURTS (STATE).  See also
Death, D 18
New York State – Elections – Courts, D 23
SURFING
 Article discusses career of surfer Mark Foo, who
drowned while surfing Pillar Point in California;
photo; map (M).  D 29,B,14:1
SURGEON GENERAL (US).  See also
Public Health Service, D 18
SURGERY and SURGEONS.  See also
Heart, D 21
SURVEILLANCE SYSTEMS.  Use Security and
Warning Systems
SURVEYS AND SERIES.  See also
Agriculture, D 28
Bombs and Bomb Plots, D 18
Crime and Criminals, D 25,26,28,29,30
Medicine and Health, D 18
Parks and Other Recreation Areas, D 26
Rwanda, D 29
United States – Congress (US), D 20
United States Armament and Defense, D 30
United States Politics and Government, D 17
```

Figure 8: An example of listings from The New York Times Index.

Other valuable research tools are guides, indexes, and registers to reference books. The merit of First Step: The Master Index to Subject Encyclopedias is evident in the title. Such a text would be able to lead you directly to something as specific as the five volume Grzimek's Encyclopedia of Mammals. You should also consult the Guide to Reference Books and the Register of Indexes.

A profoundly useful form of reference is the Citation Index. When you find a text, an essay, an article, or a report that addresses the subject you are researching, you should bring its bibliographical data to either the Arts and Literature Citation Index, the Science Citation Index, or the Social Science Citation Index (all published by the Institute for Scientific Information). If your library does not have them, find one that does. These indexes allow you to look up an article (by the author's name, then the title) and see a list of subsequent articles that have made reference to it and cited the article in their bibliographies. This gives you the opportunity to read the author's peers' published responses to his or her discovery, theory, argument, or proposal. You tap into a professional dialog on the subject you are researching. These responses give you the material to evaluate and defend your sources. The <u>Citation Indexes</u> also give an authors' sources index that lists all texts cited by an author in the bibliographies of his or her various publications. There are also subject indexes with which you might access a <u>Citation Index</u> directly.

Bibliography Cards

In conducting this research, you must make bibliography cards to keep track of all of your potential sources. Using one card per text or article, note the author's name, the title of the work, its place of publication, its publisher, and its year of publication. A special note should be made about the style of presenting titles of books, magazines, newspapers, and plays. While it is correct to either italicize or underline these titles, it is preferred to underline them because some computer printers have indistinct italics characters, or none at all. Specific formats and variants are handled as follows:

One-Author Books

Note that the author is given last name first; the full author's name is followed by a period, and then the title; the title is underlined and ends with a period; the city is stated, followed by a colon and the publisher's name; next is a comma, the year of publication, and finally a period (see Figure 9).

```
Newman, Art. The Illustrated Treasury of Medical
        Curiosa. New York: McGraw-Hill, Inc., 1988.
```

Figure 9: Sample bibliography card for a one-author book.

Two-Author Books

Note that the authors are in the order that they appear on the title page (not necessarily alphabetical order), and that the second name is given first name first.

> Colson, Charles and Jack Eckerd. Why America Doesn't Work. Dallas: Word Publishing, 1991.

Multiple-Author Books

If the book has more than three authors, the name that occurs first alphabetically is chosen to represent the group, "et al" meaning "and others."

> Adams, Raymond F. et al. The Book of the American West. New York: Simon & Schuster, 1963.

One-Editor Books

Note that the title of the editor, given as "ed.," follows the name after a comma. The period abbreviating "editor" and the other preceding the title merge into one.

> Booss, Claire, ed. A Treasury of Irish Myth, Legend, and Folklore. New York: Gramercy Books, 1986.

Note that variants for edited books change in the same pattern as authored books.

One-Translator Books

Note that translations are distinct works that can vary widely with mutual sources. List the author's name first, and place the translator's name after the book's title. Precede the translator's name with "Trans." For example:

> Chaucer, Geoffrey. The Canterbury Tales. Trans. R.M. Lumiansky. New
> York: Simon and Schuster Inc., 1954.

Note that variants for translator books change in the same pattern as authored books.

Compilation Books or Anthologies

In these, chapters are written individually by separate authors, generating the equivalent of an article. The article is the true reference, not the book as a whole, so the author of the article is more relevant than the editor of the book. The format is almost the same except for adding the article author and title to the beginning, and article titles are put in quotes rather than underlined. Add the editor's name, first name first, after the title of the book (see Figure 10).

> Christianson, John. "Lahaina Whale-Song." An Anthology of
> Polynesian Poetry and Song. Ed. Ronald Jarret. Toronto:
> University of Toronto Press, 1982.

Figure 10: Sample bibliography card for a compilation book or anthology.

Note that variants for articles in compilation books or anthologies change in the same pattern as authored books.

Periodicals

Note that periodical references take a form similar to compilation books, but omit the editors and the city of publication. Also note the addition of the volume number and more specified date of publication (see Figure 11).

```
Colley, Linda. "Women and their Political Power." The
       Wilson Quarterly, vol. XVI (Spring 1992): 31-36.
```

Figure 11: Sample bibliography card for a periodical.

Note that variants for articles in periodicals change in the same pattern as authored books.

Encyclopedia Articles

Note that encyclopedia references are similar to periodical references, but that they further omit the name of the publisher. Also, the edition number is added, after the encyclopedia name and before the year. Many encyclopedia articles are written anonymously, and so are alphabetized by the article title. For an authored encyclopedia title, include the author's name as for a periodical (see Figure 12).

"Isotope." <u>Encyclopedia Britannica</u>. 11th ed. 1966.

Figure 12: Sample bibliography card for an encyclopedia article.

Note that variants only occur for authored articles, and in those cases change in the same pattern as authored books.

Evaluating Sources

Now that you have a stack of bibliography cards of potential sources, you will find and evaluate these sources. For books, first skim the preface and table of contents to see if it truly deals with your topic. Then, the most helpful check is to look up your topic in the book's index to see how many pages are listed. The more continuous pages listed, the more informative those passages will be. Remember to use various synonyms for your topics to insure that you find all your needed information. Articles usually require skimming for evaluation, but some more scholarly journals will have indexes to check. At this hands-on stage you will have the opportunity to see how recent the edition is, and to examine the credentials of the author(s). If you find that you have bibliography cards for which you cannot find the books, keep them in case you later have access to a different library or other facility.

Notecards

Notecards are the best way to keep track of the information you find, and they will be handy as you organize and write your paper. Write a few words across the top of the card identifying its contents (see Figure 13). In the body of the card, write the idea, information, or quotation. Be sure to put only one item on each card, because two bits of information found on the same page in a source text may ultimately be on two distant pages of your term paper. Make it clear whether you are quoting directly from your source, or paraphrasing the author's words. If you are quoting, you will have to be sure and make this clear when you use the quote in your term paper, and it's best to mark this in your notes so that you do not inadvertently use the author's own words without acknowledging it. At the bottom of the card, record the author's name, the text's title, and the specific page number(s) of whatever inspired your note. This will refer you to the bibliography card that has the rest of the required citation information.

> Water Waves
>
> "... water particles move in a nearly circular path, its motion having both transverse and logitudinal components."
>
> Tipler, Physics p. 399

Figure 13: Sample notecard.

III. COMPOSING THE PAPER

The Outline and Organizing the Main Points

Making an outline is the next logical step in preparing a paper. It requires only a short time to prepare, and it helps tremendously when actually writing the paper. Writing a paper without an outline is like taking a walk through a strange city without a map. The destination might be reached, but only by chance. With a map, the traveler can know the way in advance. Similarly, an outline is a plan; it guides you through the paper by clear and logical steps.

When writing an outline, you should note all thoughts on the subject in short phrases, considering whether they contribute to the purpose and point of the paper. To return to the surfing example, you might want to explain what surfing is and why it is enjoyable. The following thoughts might occur:

> surfing is fun
> you need a board
> what the board is made of
> length and weight of the board
> how to learn
> where surfing came from
> you can surf on Long Island, but it is better in Hawaii

The next step is organization. First group the ideas. Many entries concern the board. Group them under a main heading called The Board. Then four other points remain: surfing is fun, learning to surf, history of surfing, and good places to surf. Along with The Board, these become the main points, because they cannot be grouped under any other heading. These are the major headings; all other points will fall under one of them.

These main points must be organized. The order must be logical to both you and the reader. They should develop, or work toward, an end.

The following is a sample outline for the surfing paper:

Introduction
History of surfing
The board
    why you need it
    its length and weight
    what it is made of
How to learn to surf
Surfing is fun
Best places to surf

Now, in looking over the outline, you might decide to spend the major part of the paper discussing the board and how to learn and might make the last two sections rather short. Or, you might decide to make all the sections about the same length, except the first one, which should be relatively short because it is a general introduction to the paper. Decisions of this nature should be made before any writing is attempted.

Parts of the Term Paper

The introduction should bring the reader into the paper. It should indicate the general idea of the paper (the point) and make it sound as interesting as possible. Here are some examples:

Every child can remember hearing fairy tales. Each nation on Earth has fairy tales. But strange as those stories may be, they are not as strange as the fact that fairy tales are the same the world over. They are always the same stories in different words and the same characters in different clothes.

Shakespeare's most thought-provoking play is <u>Hamlet</u>. It has given rise to more varied and contradictory interpretations than any of this other plays. One point that few can agree on is Hamlet's insanity: Was it feigned or real?

If a paper is well thought out and focused, the conclusion should be fairly easy to write. It sums up the paper, touches on the main points, and makes a final statement about the subject. It works in such a way that the reader not only feels they know what they have read, but understands the point of the paper. Not only is a conclusion a summary, it is the last part in a chain of thought or reasoning. Some sample conclusions appear below:

In spite of the bugs, the cold, the rain, and my wife's endless nagging, the trip really was a lot of fun.

We have seen that Mr. Jones' interpretation of <u>Hamlet</u> has very little to do with the play itself. Mr. Jones tells much about Sigmund Freud and his theories, but very little about Shakespeare's <u>Hamlet</u>.

Once again we see how a trivial incident can have large and unexpected consequences.

Writing the Rough Draft

Drafting is the stage in the writing process during which you use all the information gathered from prewriting and your notecards in order to write about the topic at hand. Drafting allows you to write without censorship and without worrying about the regulations and details of writing itself.

Drafting is not unlike writing a letter to a long absent friend. That's what rough drafting is: telling readers the "news," providing them with information relevant to the topic. You have completed the draft when you determine that there is nothing more to say, after having reviewed the pre-writing notes. If something is thought of later, you should add it to the draft, either at the end or, if using a computer, where it fits best. In this stage of the writing process, the writing is fast, messy, and often disorganized. This is no reason for concern. These trouble spots will be taken care of in the next stage: revising.

Revising, Editing, and Proofreading

Revising occurs each time a concept in the rough draft is changed, rearranged, or altered. Be sure to examine the organization, paragraphing, scope and nature of the point, or format (the appearance and layout of the paper). This is the step and time in the process when transitions, flow, and the logic of the paper are analyzed. Revise before editing, and remember to keep paragraphs short and concise. This may entail moving whole paragraphs from one place to another within the text, adding a transition, or cutting out whole paragraphs. Continue this process until the paper logically supports the point.

Editing is the stage after revising in which correct grammar, sentence style, diction, punctuation, and spelling are inspected. When editing a paper, focus attention not on the concepts, content, or logic, but on the clarity of sentences and the correctness of the grammar. If problems of organization and logic still exist, revise the paper more before editing. Editing should be strictly for grammar and individual sentence structure.

Proofreading is the next to last stage of the writing process. In this stage, check the paper for mechanical errors such as doubled words, mistyped (typos) words, incorrect margins, or unwanted marks of any kind. In proofreading, the goal is to "clean up" the document so that it has no typing or visual errors and is ready for the reader's eye.

After all these stages have been completed, typed, or finished, print the final copy with the proofreading changes included so that the paper is turned in as a clean copy, with absolutely no errors.

IV. PREPARING YOUR PAPER FOR PRESENTATION

The Paper, Margins, Typing, and Binding

Standardized presentation formats primarily serve to emphasize the content of term papers. When margins and citation methods are universal from paper to paper, the grader is free to examine the material being presented. Standardization of abbreviations and other shortcuts provide clarity and convenience to both you and the grader without potentially confusing explanatory keys. The assignment of a term paper is meant to test your research and reasoning, which is where all your efforts have been concentrated. Do not allow carelessness in your presentation detract from these greater labors.

Your term paper should be typed on 8-1/2 × 11-inch white paper. The paper should be of good quality, with some cotton or "rag" content for thickness. This thickness will prevent blank spaces of a page from revealing the contents of the next page, which is considered distracting even when it is too faint to read. If you are using continuous-feed paper, as many printers accept, avoid paper with distinct perforation points; most quality continuous-feed papers feature fine perforation. It is increasingly rare for papers to be accepted hand-written. Never submit a hand-written paper without explicitly being given permission to do so.

Even with such permission, a typed paper is always preferable if at all possible. If you are hand-writing your paper, use college-ruled lined paper and print as opposed to using script. All rules for presentation format will apply equally to a hand-written paper.

The margins of your paper should be 1 inch from the top, bottom, left, and right. The page numbers will be in the top margin, located at the right margin two rows of type above the first line of the page. The first page will be an exception to this format in two respects: the top margin will be three inches, and there will be no page number given. Note that footnotes, if they are placed on the same page as the reference, do not occupy the bottom margin. They obey all margins and must be planned for. In most cases it is acceptable and even preferred to bind the pages of your term paper with a single staple in the top left corner. Some graders and/or students may prefer to use a cover with a left-edge binder. When such binders are used, the left margin of the paper should be 1-1/2 inches while all other margins and rules remain unchanged.

Paper size = 8-1/2 × 11

Paper Weight = twenty pound or better

Paper Color = white

Margins
   Top = 1 inch. Use 3 inches for the first page of
        each chapter or section.

   Bottom = 1 inch

   Right = 1 inch

Left = 1-1/4 inches. Use 1-1/2 inches if your paper is to have a binder.

Spacing = doubled

Page Numbering = At the top-right margin, two rows above the first or top line. No page number on the first page.

Figure 14: Reference Table for Presentation of Paper.

The Title Page

The term paper's first sheet should be the title page. Note that this is not a cover page—illustrations and pictures are unnecessary and inappropriate. One third of the page from the top, center the title of your paper using standard book title capitalization. For longer titles, double space between lines, continue to center the lines, and distribute the words to create lines of nearly equal length. You may also apply these rules to make two lines of a longer one-line title. At the bottom right corner of the page, observing the 1-inch margins, place a single-spaced block that gives your name on the first line, the course for which the paper is required on the next one or two lines, the teacher's name on the follow-ing line, and the date on the last line (1 inch from the bottom of the page). The longest entry should dictate the starting point for the others such that all are lines up on their left side, as such:

Your Name

The Course

The Teacher

Date

The date should be given in the format of the month as a word, followed by the day of the month given as a number with a comma, and finally the year as a number, such as July 4, 1776. The date you give should generally be the due date, even when you submit your paper early (this assists identification of the assignment). If circumstances require you to submit your paper late, clarity and honesty dictate that the date on the paper should be the actual date of submission.

The Outline

Following the title page and the table of contents will be the paper's typed outline. This outline will be the one you used to organize your paper in the pre-writing stage, and therefore should accurately reflect the flow of topics through the body of the paper. An outline is a chart of subjects, branching from the general to the increasingly specific. The broadest topics are indicated with upper case roman numerals and begin at the left margins. The largest subtopics of these are placed beneath them, indented five spaces and sequenced by upper case letters. Subtopics of subtopics become increasingly narrow, continuing from subjects that are numbered with Arabic numerals, to those followed by lower case letters and finally to lower case roman numerals, each indented an additional five spaces from the left margin. Roman numerals are given extra indentation to give equally-ranked topics the same starting point at the left. Each numeral and letter marking is followed by a period and two spaces. The following fictitious biography outline demonstrates the outline format:

I. Childhood
    A. Parentage
    B. War Years
        1. hardships

                    a. poverty
                    b. family
                            i. brother enlists, dies
                            ii. parents die in bombing
                            iii. siblings distributed
              2. early accomplishments
    II. Adulthood
        A. Writing Career
              1. early struggle
              2. success
                    a. first recognition
                    b. rise to fame
              3. later works
        B. Family
              1. Marriage
              2. Offspring
        C. Death

Each topic should have either zero, two, or more subtopics. Never give an "A/a" without a "B/b" or an "I/I/i" without a "II/2/ii." When you find that you have six or more subtopics of equal rank under the same topic, stop to consider whether they should be under two different topics. Note that only the two highest subtopic rankings are capitalized, and that no level of the outline is more than a sentence fragment.

Footnotes

Footnotes acknowledge your sources of information while establishing the credibility of your materials. Failure to acknowledge sources is a crime called plagiarism, which is grounds for failure in all classrooms and expulsion at most colleges. A footnote should accompany every direct quotation, give the source of any important piece of information, and designate opinions borrowed from other writers. Another use of footnotes is to give longer parenthetic comments without interrupting the flow of the paper. These may include definitions or explanations that some readers would need and others would not. Also, if you cannot resist a tangent, placing it in a footnote may preserve the organizational integrity of your paper as a whole.

To indicate a footnote within the body of your paper, use a raised number—a superscript on a word processor, or a regular number placed at a half-line up from the rest of the text on a typewriter. Footnotes are numbered continuously from "1" up throughout the paper. The number should be placed at the end of a quotation outside the quotation marks, at the end of a paraphrased sentence, at the end of a paraphrased paragraph, or at the end of a word or phrase requiring an explanation or sparking a tangent handled in a footnote.

There are two choices for the location of your footnotes. The first is at the bottom of the page within the margins (as shown below)[1]. The second choice (which most teachers prefer) has all footnotes at the end of the paper and not on each page.

If you are going to place your footnotes at the bottom of the page and you are using a typewriter, make four or more erasable marks at half-inch intervals along the side of your paper starting at the top of the bottom margin. Keep track of how many footnote numbers occur on each page and use one mark for each note. This is just a guide—some notes will be longer than others. Separate the last line of text for that page from the footnotes with seven underscores starting from the left margin on the very next line. Then skip a line and begin your notes. Footnotes are typed single-spaced with no lines skipped between notes.

_____

1. William Shakespeare, A Midsummer Night's Dream (New York: Washington Square Press, 1993) 102.

The content of a footnote that denotes credit for a source of information or wisdom is somewhat similar to a bibliography entry, but bears an important difference. A footnote citing must accurately and specifically tell the page or pages within a source that the words or ideas are found. If your paper is properly footnoted, a reader should be able to find the source of a credited quote in a library without consulting the paper's bibliography.

Quotations and paraphrases are footnoted with the author's name, the title, and the exact page numbers of the material. All footnotes are indented three spaces and begin with the footnote number followed by a period and two spaces. Specific formats and variants are handled as follows:

One-Author Books

The author's name is followed by a comma, the title of the text underlined, the publishing data in parenthesis, the page numbers, and finally a period.

   1. J.D. Salinger, <u>The Catcher in the Rye</u> (Boston: Little, Brown Books, 1945) 100-101.
   2. George Orwell, <u>Animal Farm</u> (New York: Harcourt, Brace, Jovanovich, Inc., 1946) 205.

Note the single spacing, no skipped lines, and that author's name occurs first name first. Also, note that page numbers are not preceded by any letters or words.

Two-Author and Multiple-Author Books

Because footnotes give the first name first for all authors' names, plural author texts do not have a significant variation. They are handled as follows:

3. Chuck Colson and Jack Eckerd, Why America Doesn't Work (Dallas: Word Publishing, 1991) 60-62.

4. Ramon Adams et al., The Book of the American West (New York: Simon & Schuster, 1963) 62.

Note that unnamed authors are denoted with the Latin "et al."

One-Editor and One-Translator Books

Be sure to make the distinction between authors and editors and translators. The format remains constant, as follows:

5. Claire Booss, ed., A Treasury of Irish Myth, Legend and Folklore (New York: Gramercy Books, 1986) 304-305.

6. Frank O. Copley, trans., Cicero: On Old Age and On Friendship (New York: John Wiley & Sons, Inc., 1963) 112.

Note that the title format for the translated texts also carries over from the one-author footnote rules. Variants for these types of footnotes follow the same pattern as one-author books.

Compilation Books or Anthologies

We are required to distinguish when chapters are authored individually. The editor's name will be inserted between the book title and the publishing information as follows:

7. Janet Adelman, "Male Bonding in Shakespeare's Characters," Shakespeare's Rough Magic, eds. Peter Ericson and Coppella Kahn (New York: Dodd, 1971) 73.

Longer footnotes such as these require one to be wary when using a typewriter. Variants for these types of footnotes follow the same pattern as one-author books.

Periodicals and Encyclopedia Articles

Simple author and title references, even with the addition of editors and greater titles, will not suffice for these footnotes. Because of the nature of the sources, both require volume numbers to be cited, as follows:

8. Linda Colley, "Women and Their Political Power," The Wilson Quarterly, vol. XVI: 20-21.

9. "Isotope," Encyclopedia Britannica, 1985 ed., 311-312.

The edition reference for encyclopedias in footnotes is very important to ensure the accuracy of the page numbers.

Special Citations

Biblical, dramatic, and poetic footnote citations have special convenient forms for brevity and clarity. These will probably look familiar:

10. John 19:6.

11. William Shakespeare, Othello, V.ii.1-6.

12. William Wordsworth, "The World is Too Much With Us," ll.11-12.

See The Norton Anthology of Poetry, Third edition, shorter.

The bible format is so standard that <u>The Bible</u> is not mentioned by name, but we give the book, chapter, and verse. For plays, the author and title are followed by a series of numbers. The upper case roman numerals tell the act; the lower case numerals tell the scene within the act; and the Arabic numerals tell the lines within the scene. For poetry, we give the author, the title, and the line numbers preceded by "l." or "ll." for "line" or "lines." Poetry considered classic literature is not associated with a single text, but to be polite we give the source we used by title and edition.

Another special citation is quoting text second hand. At times, an original work is unavailable or of limited necessity. A second work that quotes the first may be used as a source for that first work, as follows:

13. William Butler Yeats, <u>Fairy and Folk Tales of the Irish Peasantry</u>, quoted in Claire Booss, ed., <u>A Treasury of Irish Myth, Legend, and Folklore</u> (New York: Gramercy Books, 1986), vii-ix.

It may seem easier to claim the Yeats text as a direct source, but remember that a reader is meant to be able to refer to your sources. The secondary source is what is available to you and must be recognized.

Repeat Footnotes

Abbreviated formats exist for second and subsequent citations of the same text. For example:

14. Salinger, 100-101.
15. Salinger, 100-101.
16. Adelman, 74-75.
17. Adelman, 78.

Here we referenced J.D. Salinger's The Catcher in the Rye pages 100-101 from footnote 1, and then referenced the same pages a third time in footnote 14. Then we referenced Janet Adelman's "Male Bonding..." article from footnote 7, but for different pages. The last reference cites a new page of Adelman's article.

If you have used two books by the same author and need to footnote both of them, the repeat footnotes will have the author's last name and a shortened form of the title of the work. For example:

18. Orwell, Animal 87.
19. Orwell, 1984 22-26.

Here we referenced George Orwell's Animal Farm page 87 from footnote 2, and then we referenced another book by Orwell, 1984 pages 22-26.

Quotations and Appendices

The format for quoting within the body of your paper varies with the length and nature of the quote. For a standard quoted sentence, put it in quotes and begin with a capital letter. For sentence fragments, use quotes, begin with a lower case letter, and maintain grammatical flow between your text and the quoted text. Text quotations longer than two lines should be introduced with a colon:

> "...and begin on the next line indented five spaces (the same as the beginning of a paragraph) and be single-spaced. The last line should end with the footnote number, just like the end of any quote."

At the end of such a quote, resume double spacing and begin the next sentence at the left margin to continue the paragraph. Note that a quote (especially an indented one) should almost never end a paragraph, because if it deserves quotation it deserves your comments.

When quoting lines of poetry or verse drama, indicate the break from line to line with a "/," such as "Look out stomach,/Here it comes!" For multiple lines, set the quotation apart like a longer text quotation by indenting and single spacing, such as:

> It is the cause, it is the cause, my soul.
> Let me not name it to you, you chaste stars.
> It is the cause. Yet I'll not shed her blood
> Nor scar that whiter skin of hers than snow,
> And smooth as monumental alabaster.
> Yet she must die, else she'll betray more men.[11]

Some may prefer to include the line numbers noted at five- or ten-line intervals for greater understanding when subsequently referring to parts of the quoted verse. These line numbers should be taken from the source, not counted as the lines occur out of context in your paper.

Any quotation that seems extremely long or repeatedly referred to may be better placed as an appendix. Footnotes for a quoted section may read "14. See Appendix A." as long as in addition to providing the passage the appendix cites the source. Other uses of appendices are to provide statistical tables and charts that support data in the paper but that do not need to be read in the continuity of the body of the paper; and to relocate longer explanatory footnotes for a neater looking body. Appendices should occur between the body of the paper and its bibliography. They should be labeled with capital letters, such as "APPENDIX B." This title should occur centered at the top line of the first page of the appendix.

Bibliography

Your paper will end with a bibliography labeled "BIBLIOGRAPHY" centered at the top line of the page. Skipping two lines, enter your single-spaced source references with one space skipped between each reference. The format for these references is exactly as described for the bibliography cards. The references should be alphabetized based upon the first word, unless an uncredited title begins with "The," "An" or "A," in which case refer to the second word. Include any source that contributed to the paper, increasing your understanding of the subject, even if the source was never quoted or paraphrased. You may decide to classify the entries to your bibliography by book, periodical, and other types of source. Another practice is to distinguish between primary readings and secondary readings. Any such classifications should be labeled and internally alphabetized.

The Final Check

Now your paper is complete. Proofread it again and have another person also proofread it. Verify that all of your sources are in your bibliography, especially those cited in your footnotes. Erase any pencil lines you may have drawn to guide your margins or footnote placement. Be sure to include the table of contents after the title page. Make sure the pages are all present, in order, and right side up. In other words, assume nothing—examine your paper with the clear mind that your grader will have. When you are confident that the paper has reached the status of "final draft," bind and submit it.

HELPFUL HINTS ON GRAMMAR AND WRITING

I. GUIDELINES FOR PUNCTUATION MARKS

End Punctuation Marks

Try to read this paragraph.

take some more tea the march hare said to alice very earnestly ive had nothing yet alice replied in an offended tone so i cant take more you mean you cant take less said the hatter its very easy to take more than nothing lewis carroll

Now try again.

"Take some more tea," the March Hare said to Alice, very earnestly.

"I've had nothing yet," Alice replied in an offended tone, "so I can't take more."

"You mean you can't take less," said the Hatter. "It's very easy to take more than nothing."

—Lewis Carroll

This example illustrates to what extent punctuation helps the reader understand what the writer is trying to say. The most important role of punctuation is clarification.

In speech, words are accompanied by gesture, voice, tone, and rhythm that help convey a desired meaning. In writing, it is punctuation alone that must do the same job.

There are many rules about how to use the various punctuation marks. These are sometimes difficult to understand, because they are described with so much grammatical terminology. Therefore, this discussion of punctuation will avoid as much terminology as possible. If you still find the rules confusing, and your method of punctuation is somewhat random, try to remember that most punctuation takes the place of pauses in speech.

Keeping this in mind, read your sentences aloud as you write; if you punctuate according to the pauses in your voice, you will do much better than if you put in your commas, periods, and dashes either at random or where they look good.

There are three ways to end a sentence.

1. a period
2. a question mark
3. an exclamation point

The Period

Periods end all sentences that are not questions or exclamations. In speech, the end of a sentence is indicated with a full pause. The period is the written counterpart of this pause.

Go get me my paper. I'm anxious to see the news.
Into each life some rain must fall. Last night some fell into mine.

When a question is intended as a suggestion and the listener is not expected to answer or when a question is asked indirectly as part of a sentence, a period is also used.

Mimi wondered if the parade would ever end.
Will you please send the flowers you advertised.
We'll never know who the culprit was.

Periods also follow most abbreviations and contractions.

Wed.	Dr.	Jr.	Sr.
etc.	Jan.	Mr.	Mrs.
Esq.	cont.	a.m.	A.D.

Periods (or parentheses) are also used after a letter or number in a series.

a. apples   1. president
b. oranges   2. vice president
c. pears   3. secretary

Errors to Avoid:

Be sure to omit the period after a quotation mark preceded by a period. Only one stop is necessary to end a sentence.

She said, "Hold my hand." (no period after the final quotation mark)

"Don't go into the park until later."

"It's not my fault," he said. "She would have taken the car anyway."

After many abbreviations, particularly those of organizations or agencies, no period is used (check in a dictionary if in doubt).

AFL-CIO   NAACP   GM
FBI   NATO   IBM
TV   UN   HEW

The Question Mark

Use a question mark to end a direct question even if it is not in the form of a question. The question mark in writing denotes the rising tone of voice used to indicate a question in speech. If you read the following two sentences aloud, you will see the difference in tone between a statement and a question composed of the same words.

Mary is here.
Mary is here?

Here are some more examples of correct use of the question mark. Pay special attention to the way it is used with other punctuation.

Where will we go next?

"Won't you," he asked, "please lend me a hand?"

"Will they ever give us our freedom?" the prisoner asked.

Who asked, "When?"

Question marks indicate a full stop and lend a different emphasis to a sentence than do commas. Compare these pairs of sentences.

Was the sonata by Beethoven? or Brahms? or Chopin?

Was the sonata by Beethoven, or Brahms, or Chopin?

Did they walk to the park? climb the small hill? take the bus to town? or go skating out back?

Did they walk to town, climb the small hill, take the bus to town, or go skating out back?

Sometimes question marks are placed in parentheses. This indicates doubt or uncertainty about the facts being reported.

The bombing started at 3 a.m.(?)

She said the dress cost $200,000.(?)

Harriet Stacher (18(?)-1914) was well thought of in her time.

Hippocrates (460(?)-(?)377 B.C.) is said to be the father of modern medicine.

The Exclamation Point

An exclamation point ends an emphatic statement. It should be used only to express strong emotions, such as surprise, disbelief, or admiration. If it is used too often for mild expressions of emotion, it loses its effectiveness.

Let go of me!

Help! Fire!

It was a wonderful day!

What a beautiful woman she is!

Who shouted "Fire!" *(Notice no question mark is necessary)*

Fantastic!

"Unbelievable!" she gasped. *(Notice no comma is necessary)*

"You'll never win!" he cried.

Where else can I go! *(The use of the exclamation point shows that this is a strong statement even though it is worded like a question.)*

Do not overuse exclamation points. The following is an example of the overuse of exclamation points:

Dear Susan,

    I was so glad to see you last week! You looked better than ever! Our talk meant so much to me! I can hardly wait until we get together again! Could you believe how long it has been! Let's never let that happen again! Please write as soon as you get the chance! I can hardly wait to hear from you!

                           Your friend,

                           Nora

Interjections

An interjection is a word or group of words used as an exclamation to express emotion. It need not be followed by an exclamation point. Often an interjection is followed by a comma (see *The Comma*) if it is not very intense. Technically, the interjection has no grammatical relation to other words in the sentence; yet it is still considered a part of speech.

Oh dear, I forgot my keys again.

Ah! Now do you understand?

Ouch! I didn't realize that the stove was hot.

Oh, excuse me. I didn't realize that you were next on line.

INTERNAL PUNCTUATION MARKS

The Comma

Of all the marks of punctuation, the comma (,) has the most uses. Before you tackle the main principles that guide its usage, be sure that you have an elementary understanding of sentence structure. There are actually only a few rules and conventions to follow when using commas; the rest is common sense. The worst abuse of commas comes from those who overuse them or who place them illogically. If you are ever in doubt as to whether or not to use a comma, do not use it.

In A Series

When more than one adjective (an adjective series) describes a noun, use a comma to separate and emphasize each adjective.

the long, dark passageway

another confusing, sleepless night

an elaborate, complex plan

In these instances, the comma takes the place of "and." To test if the comma is needed, try inserting "and" between the adjectives in question. If it is logical, you should use a comma. The following are examples of adjectives that describe an adjective-noun combination that has come to be thought of almost as one word. In such cases, the adjective in front of the adjective-noun combination needs no comma.

a stately *oak tree*   my worst *report card*

an exceptional *wine glass*   a borrowed *record player*

a successful *garage sale*   a porcelain *dinner plate*

If you insert "and" between the adjectives in the above examples, it will not make sense.

The comma is also used to separate words, phrases, and whole ideas (clauses); it still takes the place of "and" when used this way.

an apple, a pear, a fig, and a banana

a lovely lady, an indecent dress, and many admirers

She lowered the shade, closed the curtain, turned off the light, and went to bed.

John, Frank, and my Uncle Harry all thought it was a questionable theory.

The only question that exists about the use of commas in a series is whether or not one should be used before the final item. Usually "and" or "or" precedes the final item, and many writers do not include the comma before the final "and" or "or." However, it is advisable to use the comma, because often its omission can be confusing—in such cases as these, for instance.

NO: Would you like to shop at Sak's, Lord and Taylor's and Macy's?

NO: He got on his horse, tracked a rabbit and a deer and rode on to Canton.

NO: We planned the trip with Mary and Harold, Susan, Dick and Joan, Gregory and Jean and Charles. *(Is it Gregory and Jean or Jean and Charles or Gregory and Jean and Charles?)*

Introductory Words, Phrases, and Clauses

Usually if a phrase or clause precedes the subject at the beginning of a sentence, a comma is used to set it off.

After last night's fiasco at the disco, she couldn't bear the thought of looking at him again. (introductory phrase)

Whenever I try to talk about politics, my husband leaves the room. (introductory clause)

If an introductory phrase includes a verb form that is being used as another part of speech (a "verbal"), it must be followed by a comma. Introductory elliptical clauses must also be followed by a comma. Try to make sense of the following sentences without commas.

NO: When eating Mary never looked up from her plate.

YES: When eating, Mary never looked up from her plate. (elliptical clause)

NO: Because of her desire to follow her faith in James wavered.

YES: Because of her desire to follow, her faith in James wavered.

Above all, common sense is the best guideline when trying to decide whether or not to use a comma after an introductory phrase. Does the comma make the meaning clearer? If it does, use it; if not, there is no reason to insert it.

To Separate Sentences with Two Main Ideas (Compound Sentences)

To understand this use of the comma, you need to have studied sentence structure and be able to recognize compound sentences.

When a sentence contains more than two subjects and verbs (clauses) and the two clauses are joined by a connecting word (*and*, *but*, *or*, *yet*, *for*, *nor*), use a comma before the connecting word to show that another clause is coming.

I thought I knew the poem by heart, but he showed me three lines I had forgotten.

Are we really interested in helping the children, or are we more concerned with protecting our good names?

If the two parts of the sentence are short and closely related, it is not necessary to use a comma.

He threw the ball and the dog ran after it.

Jane played the piano and Charles danced.

Errors to Avoid:

Be careful not to confuse a compound sentence with a sentence that has a compound verb and a single subject. If the subject is the same for both verbs, there is no need for a comma.

> NO: Charles sent some flowers, and wrote a long letter explaining why he had not been able to come.

> NO: Last Thursday we went to the concert with Julia, and afterward dined at an old Italian restaurant.

With Interrupting Material

There are so many different kinds of interruptions that can occur in a sentence that a list of them all would be quite lengthy. In general, words and phrases that stop the flow of the sentence or are unnecessary for the main idea are set off by commas.

Abbreviations after names
Did you invite John Paul, Jr., and his sister?

Interjections: An exclamation added without grammatical connection.
Oh, I'm so glad to see you.

Direct address
Roy, won't you open the door for the dog?
I can't understand, Mother, what you are trying to say.

Tag questions: A question that repeats the helping verb and is in the negative.

I'm really hungry, aren't you?

Jerry looks like his father, doesn't he?

Geographical names and addresses

The concert will be held in Chicago, Illinois, on August 12.

The letter was addressed to Ms. Marion Heartwell, 1881 Pine Lane, Palo Alto, California 95824. *(No comma is used before a zip code.)*

Transitional words and phrases

On the other hand, I hope he gets better.

You'll find, therefore, no one more loyal to you than I.

Parenthetical words and phrases

You will become, I believe, a great statesman.

We know, of course, that this is the only thing to do.

Unusual word order

The dress, new and crisp, hung in the closet. *(Normal word order: The new, crisp dress hung in the closet.)*

Intently, she stared out the window. *(Normal word order: She stared intently out the window.)*

With Nonrestrictive Elements (Not Essential to the Meaning)

Parts of a sentence that modify other parts are sometimes essential to the meaning of the sentence and sometimes not. When a modifying word or group of words is not vital to the meaning of the sentence, it is set off by commas. Since it does not restrict the meaning of the words it modifies, it is called "nonrestrictive."

Modifiers that are essential to the meaning of the sentence are called "restrictive" and are not set off by commas. Compare the following pairs of sentences:

The girl *who wrote the story* is my sister. (essential)

My sister, *the girl who wrote the story*, has always been drawn to adventure. (nonessential)

The cup *that is on the piano* is the one I want. (essential)

The cup, *which my brother gave me last year*, is on the piano. (nonessential)

She always listened to her sister *Jean*. (essential—she must have more than one sister)

She always listened to her husband, *Jack*. (nonessential—obviously, she has only one husband)

With Direct Quotations

Most direct quotes or quoted materials are set off from the rest of the sentence by commas.

"Please read your part more loudly," the director insisted.

"I won't know what to do," said Michael, "if you leave me now."

Mark looked up from his work, smiled, and said, "We'll be with you in a moment."

Be careful not to set off indirect quotations or quotes that are used as subjects or complements.

"To be or not to be" is the famous beginning of a soliloquy in Shakespeare's *Hamlet*. (subject)

Back then my favorite song was "A Summer Place." (complement)

She said she would never come back. (indirect quote)

With Contrasting Elements

Her intelligence, *not her beauty*, got her the job.

Your plan will take you further from, *rather than closer to*, your destination.

<u>With Dates</u>

Both forms of the date are acceptable.

She will arrive on April 6, 1995.

He left on 5 December 1994.

In January 1995 he handed in his resignation.

In January, 1995, he handed in his resignation.

The Semicolon

Semicolons (;) are sometimes called mild periods. They indicate a pause midway in length between the comma and the colon. Writing that contains many semicolons is usually in a dignified, formal style. To use them correctly, it is necessary to be able to recognize main clauses—complete ideas. When two main clauses occur in a single sentence without a connecting word (*and, but, or, nor, for*), the appropriate mark of punctuation is the semicolon.

It is not a good idea for you to leave the country right now; you should actually try to stay as long as you possibly can.

In the past, boy babies were often dressed in blue; girls, in pink. *("Were often dressed" is understood in the second part of the sentence.)*

Burgundy and maroon are very similar colors; scarlet is altogether different.

Notice how the use of the comma, period, and semicolon gives a sentence a slightly different meaning.

Music lightens life; literature deepens it.

Just as music lightens life, literature deepens it.

Music lightens life. Literature deepens it.

The semicolon lends a certain balance to writing that would otherwise be difficult to achieve. Nonetheless, you should be careful not to overuse it. A comma can just as well join parts of a sentence with two main ideas; the semicolon is particularly appropriate if there is a striking contrast in the two ideas expressed.

> Ask not what your country can do for you; ask what you can do for your country.

> It started out as an ordinary day; it ended being the most extraordinary of her life.

If any one of the following words or phrases is used to join together compound sentences, it is generally preceded by a semicolon.

then	however	thus	furthermore
hence	indeed	consequently	also
that is	nevertheless	anyhow	in addition
in fact	on the other hand	likewise	moreover
still	meanwhile	instead	besides
otherwise	in other words	henceforth	for example
therefore	at the same time	even now	nonetheless

> For a long time, people thought that women were inferior to men; *even now* it is not an easy attitude to overcome.

> Being clever and cynical, he succeeded in becoming president of the company; *meanwhile*, his wife left him.

> Cigarette smoking has never interested me; *furthermore*, I couldn't care less if anyone else smokes or not.

When a series of complicated items is listed or if there is internal punctuation in a series, the semicolon is sometimes used to make the meaning clearer.

> You can use your new car for many things: to drive to town or to the country; to impress your friends and neighbors; to protect yourself from rain on a trip away from home; and to borrow against should you need money right away.

> The scores from yesterday's games came in late last night: Pirates-6, Zoomers-3; Caterpillars-12, Steelys-8; Crashers-9, Links-8; and Greens-15, Uptowns-4.

The semicolon is placed outside quotation marks or parentheses, unless it is a part of the material enclosed in those marks.

I used to call him "my lord and master"; it made him laugh every time.

The weather was cold for that time of year (I was shivering wherever I went); nevertheless, we set out to hike to the top of that mountain.

The Colon

The colon (:) is the sign of a pause about midway in length between the semicolon and the period. It can often be replaced by a comma and sometimes by a period. Although used less frequently now than it was 50 to 75 years ago, the colon is still convenient to use, for it signals to the reader that more information is to come on the subject of concern. The colon can also create a slight dramatic tension.

It is used to introduce a word, a phrase, or a complete statement (clause) that emphasizes, illustrates, or exemplifies what has already been stated.

He had only one desire in life: to play baseball.

The weather that day was the most unusual I'd ever seen: it snowed and rained while the sun was still shining.

Since the colon is not an end mark (used to end a sentence), do not capitalize after the colon unless the word is a proper noun.

May I offer you a suggestion: don't drive without your seat belts fastened.

The thought continued to perplex him: where will I go next?

When introducing a series that illustrates or emphasizes what has already been stated, use the colon.

Only a few of the graduates were able to be there: Jamison, Mearns, Linkley, and Commoner.

For Omar Khayyam, a Persian poet, three things are necessary for a paradise on earth: a loaf of bread, a jug of wine, and one's beloved.

Long quotations set off from the rest of the text by indentation rather than quotation marks are generally introduced with a colon.

The first line of Lincoln's Gettysburg address is familiar to most Americans:

Four score and seven years ago our fathers brought forth on this continent a new nation, conceived in liberty and dedicated to the proposition that all men are created equal.

I quote from Shakespeare's *Sonnets*:

When I do count the clock that tells the time,
And see the brave day sunk in hideous night;
When I behold the violet past prime,
And sable curls all silver'd o'er with white…

It is also customary to begin a business letter with a colon.

Dear Senator Jordan:

To Whom It May Concern:

Gentlemen:

Dear Sir or Madam:

In informal letters, use a comma.

Dear Mary,

Dear Father,

The colon is also used in introducing a list.

Please send the following:

1. 50 index cards

2. 4 typewriter ribbons

3. 8 erasers

Prepare the recipe as follows:

1. Slice the oranges thinly.

2. Arrange them in a circle around the strawberries.

3. Pour the liqueur over both fruits.

At least three ladies will have to be there to help:

1. Mrs. Goldman, who will greet the guests;

2. Harriet Sacher, who will serve the lunch; and

3. my sister, who will do whatever else needs to be done.

Finally, the colon is used between numbers when writing the time, between the volume and number or volume and page number of a journal, and between the chapter and verse in the Bible.

4:30 P.M.

The Nation, 34:8

Genesis 5:18

The Dash

Use the dash (—) to indicate a sudden or unexpected break in the normal flow of the sentence. It can also be used in place of parentheses or of commas if the meaning is clarified. Usually the dash gives special emphasis to the material it sets off. On a typewriter, two hyphens (—) indicate a dash.

Could you—I hate to ask!—help me with these boxes?

When we left town—a day never to be forgotten—they had a record snowfall.

She said—we all heard it—"The safe is not locked."

A dash is often used to summarize a series of ideas that have already been expressed.

Freedom of speech, freedom to vote, and freedom of assembly—these are the cornerstones of democracy.

Carbohydrates, fats, and proteins—these are the basic kinds of food we need.

The dash is also used to note the author of a quotation that is set off in the text.

Nothing is good or bad but thinking makes it so.

—William Shakespeare

Parentheses

To set off material that is only loosely connected to the central meaning of the sentence, use parentheses [( )].

Most men (at least, most that I know) like wine, women, and song but have too much work and not enough time for such enjoyments.

On Tuesday evenings and Thursday afternoons (the times I don't have classes), the television programs are not too exciting.

Watch out for other punctuation when you use parentheses. Punctuation that refers to the material enclosed in the parentheses occurs inside the marks. Punctuation belonging to the rest of the sentence comes outside the parentheses.

I thought I knew the poem by heart (boy, was I wrong!).

For a long time (too long as far as I'm concerned), women were thought to be inferior to men.

We must always strive to tell the truth. (Are we even sure we know what truth is?)

When I first saw a rose (don't you think it's the most beautiful flower?), I thought it must be man-made.

Quotation Marks

The proper use of quotation marks must be studied and learned, because some of their uses appear arbitrary and outside common sense.

The most common use of double quotation marks (" ") is to set off quoted words, phrases, and sentences.

"If everybody minded their own business," said the duchess in a hoarse growl, "the world would go round a great deal faster than it does."

"Then you would say what you mean," the March Hare went on.

"I do," Alice hastily replied: "At least—at least I mean what I say—that's the same thing, you know."

"Not the same thing a bit!" said the Hatter. "Why, you might just as well say that 'I see what I eat' is the same thing as 'I eat what I see'!"

from Lewis Carroll's

Alice in Wonderland

In the last sentence, single quotation marks are used to set off quoted material within a quote. Other examples of correct use of single quotation marks:

"Shall I bring 'Rime of the Ancient Mariner' along with us?" she asked her brother.

Mrs. Green said, "The doctor told me, 'Go immediately to bed when you get home.'"

With Commas and Periods

Remember that commas and periods are always placed inside quotation marks even if they are not actually part of the quote.

NO: "Get down here right away", John cried. "You'll miss the sunset if you don't".

YES: "Get down here right away," John cried. "You'll miss the sunset if you don't."

NO: "If my dog could talk", Mary mused, "I'll bet he would say 'Take me for a walk right this minute.'"

YES: "If my dog could talk," Mary mused, "I'll bet he would say 'Take me for a walk right this minute.'"

With Question Marks and Exclamation Points

Other marks of punctuation, such as question marks, exclamation points, colons, and semicolons, go inside the quotation marks if they are part of the quoted material. If they are not part of the quote, however, they go outside the quotation marks. Be careful to distinguish between the guidelines for the comma and period, which *always* go inside the quotation marks, and those for the other marks of punctuation.

NO: Did you hear her say, "He'll be there early?" *(The question mark belongs to the entire sentence and not to the quote alone.)*

YES: Did you hear her say, "He'll be there early"?

NO: She called down the stairs, "When are you coming"? *(The question mark belongs to the quote.)*

YES: She called down the stairs, "When are you coming?"

NO: "Ask not what your country can do for you"; said Kennedy, "ask what you can do for your country:" a statement of genius I think. *(The semicolon is part of the quoted material; the colon is not part of the quote but belongs to the entire sentence.)*

YES: "Ask not what your country can do for you;" said Kennedy, "ask what you can do for your country": a statement of genius, I think.

NO: "Let me out"! he cried. "Don't you have any pity"?

YES: "Let me out!" he cried. "Don't you have any pity?"

Remember to use only one mark of punctuation at the end of a sentence ending with a quotation.

NO: She thought aloud, "Will I ever finish this paper in time for that class?".

YES: She thought aloud, "Will I ever finish this paper in time for that class?"

NO: "Not the same thing a bit!", said the Hatter. "Why, you might just as well say that 'I see what I eat' is the same thing as 'I eat what I see'!".

YES: "Not the same thing a bit!" said the Hatter. "Why, you might just as well say that 'I see what I eat' is the same thing as 'I eat what I see'!"

Writing Dialogue

When writing dialogue, begin a new paragraph each time the speaker changes.

"Do you know what time it is?" asked Jane. "I don't want to be late for my class."

"Can't you see I'm busy?" snapped Mary. "Go into the kitchen if you want the time."

"It's easy to see you're in a bad mood today," replied Jane.

Use quotation marks to enclose words used as words. Sometimes italics are used for this purpose.

"*Judgment*" had always been a difficult word for me to spell.

I always thought "*nice*" meant "*particular*" or "*having exacting standards,*" but I know now it has acquired a much more general and vague meaning.

If slang is used within more formal writing, the slang words or phrases should be set off with quotation marks.

The "*old boy*" system is responsible for most promotions in today's corporate world.

Harrison's decision to leave the conference and to "*stick his neck out*" by flying to Jamaica was applauded by the rest of the participants.

When words are meant to have an unusual or special significance to the reader, for instance irony or humor, they are sometimes placed in quotation marks. This is, however, a practice to be avoided whenever possible. The reader should be able to get the intended meaning from the context.

For years, women were not allowed to buy real estate in order to "protect" them from unscrupulous dealers. *(The writer is using somebody else's word; the use of the quotation marks shows he or she does not believe women needed protection.)*

The "*conversation*" resulted in one black eye and a broken arm.

To set off titles of radio and TV shows, poems, stories, and chapters in a book, use quotation marks. (Book, motion picture, newspaper, and magazine titles are underlined.)

The article "Moving South in the Southern Rain," by Jergen Smith in the *Southern News*, attracted the attention of our editor.

My favorite essay by Montaigne is "On Silence."

You will find Keats' "Ode on a Grecian Urn" in chapter 3, "The Romantic Era," in Lastly's *Selections from Great English Poets*.

Errors to Avoid:

Be sure to remember that quotation marks always come in pairs. Do not make the mistake of using only one set.

NO: "You'll never convince me to move to the city, said Thurman. I consider it an insane asylum."

YES: "You'll never convince me to move to the city," said Thurman. "I consider it an insane asylum."

When a quote consists of several sentences, do not put the quotation marks at the beginning and the end of each sentence; put them at the beginning and end of the entire quotation.

NO: "It was during his student days in Bonn that Beethoven fastened upon Schiller's poem." "The heady sense of liberation in the verses must have appealed to him." "They appealed to every German."

—John Burke

YES: "It was during his student days in Bonn that Beethoven fastened upon Schiller's poem. The heady sense of liberation in the verses must have appealed to him. They appealed to every German."

—John Burke

Instead of setting off a long quote with quotation marks, you may want to indent and single space it. If you do indent, do not use quotation marks.

We are not enemies, but friends. We must not be enemies. Though passion may have strained, it must not break, our bonds of affection. The mystic chords of memory, stretching from every battlefield and patriot grave to every living heart and hearthstone all over this broad land, will yet swell the chorus of the Union when again touched, as surely they will be, by the better angels of our nature.

—Abraham Lincoln, First Inaugural Address

Be careful not to use quotation marks with indirect quotations.

NO: Mary wondered "if she would ever get over it."

YES: Mary wondered if she would ever get over it.

NO: "My exercise teacher told me," Mary said, "'that I should do these back exercises 15 minutes each day.'"

YES: "My exercise teacher told me," Mary said, "that I should do these back exercises 15 minutes each day."

When you quote several paragraphs, it is not sufficient to place quotation marks at the beginning and end of the entire quote. Place quotation marks *at the beginning of each paragraph, but at the end of only the last paragraph.* Here is an abbreviated quotation for an example.

"Here begins an odyssey through the world of classical mythology, starting with the creation of the world, proceeding to the divinities that once governed all aspects of human life.

"It is true that themes similar to the classical may be found in almost any corpus of mythology. Even technology is not immune to the influence of Greece and Rome.

"We hardly need mention the extent to which painters and sculptors have used and adapted classical mythology to illustrate the past, to reveal the human body, to express romantic or antiromantic ideals, or to symbolize any particular point of view."

The Apostrophe

To Indicate Omission

Use the apostophe to form contractions and to indicate that letters or figures have been omitted.

can't (cannot)	o'clock (of the clock)
I'll (I will)	it's (it is)
memories of '42 (1942)	won't (will not)
you've (you have)	they're (they are)

Notice that the apostrophe is *always* placed where a letter or letters have been omitted. Avoid such careless errors as writing wo'nt instead of won't, for example. Contractions are generally not used in formal writing. They are found primarily in speech and informal writing.

To Indicate the Plural Form

An apostrophe is also used to indicate the plural form of letters, figures, and words that normally don't take a plural form. In such cases it might be confusing to add only an "s."

He quickly learned his *i*'s and *s*'s.

Most of the *Ph.D.'s* and *M.D.'s* understand the new technology they are using for anticancer drugs.

Her *2's* always looked like her *4's*.

Marion used too many *the's* and *and's* in her last paper for English literature.

Whenever possible, try to form plurals by adding only "s" to numbers and to single or multiple letters used as words.

the ABCs	the 1940s
in threes and fours	three Rs

To Indicate Possession

In spoken English, the same pronunciation is used for the plural, singular possessive, and plural possessive of most nouns. It is only in context that the listener is able to tell the difference in the words used by the speaker. In written English, spelling as well as context tells readers the meaning of the noun the writer is using. The writer has only to master the placement of the apostrophe so that the meaning is clearly conveyed to the reader. These words are pronounced alike but have different meanings.

PLURAL	*SINGULAR POSSESSIVE*	*PLURAL POSSESSIVE*
neighbors	neighbor's	neighbors'
doctors	doctor's	doctors'
weeks	week's	weeks'
sopranos	soprano's	sopranos'
civilizations	civilization's	civilizations'

If you aren't sure of the apostrophe's placement, you can determine it accurately by this simple test: change the possessive phrase into "belonging to" or into an "of" phrase to discover the basic noun. You will find this a particularly useful trick for some of the more confusing possessive forms, such as those on words that end in "s" or "es."

Keats' poem: The poem belonging to Keats. Base noun is *Keats*; possessive is Keats' or Keats's, not Keat's or Keatsies.

The Joneses' house: The house of the Joneses (plural of Jones). Base is *Joneses*; possessive is Joneses', not Jones' or Jones'es.

Four months' pay: The pay of four months. *Months* is base; possessive is months', not month's.

The lioness' strength: The strength of the lioness. *Lioness* is base; possessive is lioness' or lioness's, not lioness'es or liones's.

It is anybody's guess: The guess of anybody. *Anybody* is the base noun; possessive is anybody's, not anybodys' or anybodies'.

Italics

Italic is a particular kind of type used by printers. It is a light, thin type that slants to the right. In writing or typing, italic is indicated by underlining. Although its usage varies a great deal, there are some general guidelines that should be followed.

Italics are used most often to indicate the title of a play, book, movie, long poem, newspaper, magazine, musical composition, work of art, ship, train, or aircraft.

She had just read Kenneth Clark's *Civilization*.

Leonardo da Vinci's most famous painting must certainly be *La Gioconda* which we know as the Mona Lisa. (Traditional titles or nicknames are not underlined.)

The *New York Times* (or New York *Times*) may be the best paper in the world. (The name of the city associated with a newspaper and considered part of the title may or may not be italicized.)

The *Enola Gay* dropped the first atomic bomb on Hiroshima.

Note: When the overall text is italicized (as in the sentence below), the word that would otherwise be italicized should be in roman (straight) type to better indicate the contrast.

The Enola Gay *dropped the first atomic bomb on Hiroshima.*

Errors to Avoid:

Reserve the use of quotation marks for short parts of longer works, such as stories, poems, and chapters, and for the titles of radio and TV shows. This helps distinguish the title of a book from a chapter, the name of an article from a magazine title, and a poem from the collection in which it appears.

NO: *The Southern Predicament that ran in the Atlantic Monthly* in February received attention from us all.

YES: "The Southern Predicament" that ran in the *Atlantic Monthly* in February received attention from us all.

NO: Chapter 6, *The Marijuana Question*, seems to me the most controversial part of *Drugs Today* by Himmel.

YES: Chapter 6, "The Marijuana Question," seems to me the most controversial part of *Drugs Today* by Himmel.

Use italics to indicate a foreign word that has not yet become part of accepted English. Refer to your dictionary in order to be sure of the status of a particular word. Examples of familiar foreign words that are already part of our language and that *should not be italicized are*

a priori	psyche	status quo
cliché	élan	ad hoc
staccato	trattoria	andante
fait accompli	ipso facto	rendezvous
tête-à-tête	dolce vita	

Some foreign phrases and words that should be italicized are

The Perellis all called "*arrivederci*," as Daniel left. (Italian for "farewell")

She'd always had a *femme de chambre*. (French for "chambermaid")

When words are referred to as words, then either quotation marks or italics can be used. (See *Quotation Marks*)

I'm never sure whether to use "*infer*" or "*imply*."

OR

I'm never sure whether to use infer or imply.

My "2's" and "4's" look similar.

OR

My *2's* and *4's* look similar.

Sometimes special emphasis is put on a word or phrase by underlining, italicizing, or placing it in quotation marks. Minimize this practice whenever you can; try to indicate emphasis by word order or syntax, rather than by excessive underlining, which reflects laziness on the part of the writer.

She didn't ask John to come; she asked *me*.

It's *time* that heals our wounds.

Hyphens

Compound Words

There are literally hundreds of rules for the use of hyphens—especially in compound words. The following are some of the most important, more dependable rules for hyphenation of compounds.

Hyphenate two or more words used as adjectives when you want to express the idea of a unit, if they come before the word they modify. If, however, they follow the main word, they should generally not be hyphenated. (See *Adjectives and Adverbs*.)

well-known man	a man who is well known
twelve-foot ceiling	a ceiling of twelve feet

| up-to-date information | he is up to date |
| on-the-job training | training is on the job |

There are exceptions. Some compound adjectives retain the hyphen even if they follow the word they modify. Some you should know are

All words (nouns and adjectives) that start with "self":

self-reliant boy	he is self-reliant
self-supporting girl	she is self-supporting
self-cleaning oven	it is self-cleaning

All adjective compounds that start with "all":

| all-encompassing book | the book is all-encompassing |

All adjectival compounds that start with "half":

half-done cake	cake was half-done
half-awake student	student was half-awake
half-explored territory	territory is only half-explored

Compound adjectives that use "ly" are not hyphenated before or after the word they modify.

| highly developed muscles | his muscles were highly developed |
| interestingly formed rocks | rocks that are interestingly formed |

In general, compound words that serve as nouns are not hyphenated. Compare:

Problem solving (noun) was his talent.

He had a *problem-solving* (adjective) talent.

Mary is a *foster child*. (noun)

She lives at the *foster-child* (adjective) home.

Exceptions:

All "in-laws" take a hyphen.

brother-in-law   mother-in-law   sisters-in-law

In addition, hyphens have other uses, as follows:

In a series of hyphenated words with a common ending, hyphens are carried over so it is not necessary to repeat the word each time.

Is it a 100- or 200-page book?

Do you want a two-, three-, or five-column page?

They took six- and eight-cylinder cars along.

Both pro- and anti-American sentiment mounted.

Numbers from 21 to 99 are hyphenated when they are spelled out.

eighty-eight

sixty-three

two hundred forty-four

A hyphen is used to mean "up to and including" when used between numbers and dates.

1965-75   There will be 10-15 people.

the academic year 1992-93

A hyphen is also used to avoid ambiguity when two capitalized names stand together.

the Boston-New York game

the Chicago-London flight

the Kramer-Lewis debate

the Harrison-Jones marriage

Many words still have prefixes that are set off by hyphens.

pre-engineering   ex-wife (*always set "ex" off*)

pro-German   semi-independent

anti-Nixon (*prefixes added to proper nouns should always be hyphenated*)

Brackets

Brackets are probably the least used form of the pause. They do, however, serve some very useful purposes in clarifying material. When an editor needs to add corrections, explanations, or comments, brackets are used.

"They [the Murphys] never meant to send that message to the White House." (Without the bracketed words, the reader would not know who had sent the message.)

Morris continued, "After the treaty was signed [The Treaty of Versailles], jubilation filled their hearts."

The *Times* printed the senator's speech, which was addressed to "my countrymen, my countywomen [sic]." (The term [sic] indicates that the error is in the original source quoted; in this case "countywomen" should have been "countrywomen.")

Brackets are also used to avoid confusion when it is necessary to use parentheses inside of parentheses.

Darkness fell so rapidly that she and her companion (June Morrison, who had herself traveled throughout Africa [particularly Nigeria]) hardly noticed the transition from crystal blue to black.

We know of a number of scholars who disagree with this theory (see Jackson Hewitt, *To Earth's Center* [Boston: Inkwell Press, 1953], p. 614).

Ellipsis

Ellipsis (three dots:...) is used to show that words not essential to the meaning of the sentence have been omitted. A fourth dot/period is necessary when the omitted material comes at the end of a sentence.

"Fourscore and seven years ago, our fathers brought forth upon this continent a new nation,..."

"I pledge allegiance to the flag of the United States of America ...one nation under God..."

II. COMMON SENTENCE ERRORS

Dangling Modifiers

The dangling modifier is the most bizarre and comical of all sentence errors. Because it is such a glaring error, it stops readers dead in their tracks. The sentence lacks clarity, and the reader must take a moment to determine the writer's intention. The most common kind of dangling modifier is the dangling participle.

NO: At age six, my father taught me to swim.

YES: When I was six, my father taught me to swim.

NO: After showing the experiment, it was time to go home.

YES: After he showed us the experiment, we had to go home.

NO: The door was shut while dancing with Debbie.

YES: The door was shut while I was dancing with Debbie.

The difficulty with the sentences above is that the reader is not sure who is doing what. *"The door was shut while dancing with Debbie"* is ambiguous. *Who* is dancing with Debbie? The door? It is important to be clear about the sense of every sentence. Meaning can be completely changed when a word or phrase is moved into or out of the proper place.

Modifiers (participles, infinitives, and gerunds—verbals) usually dangle because, as in some of the examples above, the verbal is in search of a subject to modify.

Misplaced Modifiers

There are other types of modifiers that cause confusion when they are out of place. It is not important to learn the names of the various errors one could make, but it is important to avoid such errors. In general, structure a sentence logically by placing the modifier near the word it modifies. In each of the following examples, a phrase is out of place.

NO: I saw two stores and a movie theater walking down the street.

YES: Walking down the street, I saw two stores and a movie theater.

NO: Harold watched the painter gaping in astonishment.

YES: Harold watched the painter and gaped in astonishment.

               Gaping in astonishment, Harold watch the painter.

NO: You can see the moon standing in the front yard.

YES: If you stand in the front yard, you can see the moon.

               Standing in the front yard, you can see the moon.

There are some words that must always be placed immediately before the word they modify, or they will cause confusion. These are words like *almost, only, just, even, hardly, nearly, not,* and *merely.*

NO: Jane almost polished the plate until it shined.

YES: Jane polished the plate until it almost shined.

NO: The store on the corner only sells that toaster.

YES: Only the store on the corner sells that toaster.

Look at how the meaning can change when the modifier is moved around in the following series of sentences.

Only life exists on earth. *(There is nothing else on earth except life.)*

Life only exists on earth. *(Life does nothing but exist on earth.)*

Life exists only on earth. *(Nowhere else but on earth can one find life.)*

Life exists on earth only. *(More emphatic than the last sentence but says the same thing.)*

Place *only* and other modifiers close to the word that they modify. This is the best way to avoid ambiguity.

Split Infinitives

A split infinitive occurs when a modifier is placed between the sign of the infinitive "to" and the verb (*to better serve you*). In the italicized example, the infinitive "to serve" is split by the adverb "better." Careful writers try to avoid splitting infinitives.

Try to *not* split an infinitive.

The patient hopes to *fully* recover from pneumonia.

We want to *better* serve you.

Squinting Modifiers

A squinting modifier is one which is ambiguous because it is not clear whether it refers to the noun preceding it or the one following it.

NO: Women who like him sometimes gave him gifts.

YES: Women who like him gave him gifts sometimes.

NO: The professor sees juniors only on Fridays.

YES: The professor sees only juniors on Fridays.

Lack of Parallel Structure

When ideas are similar, they should be expressed in similar forms. When elements of a sentence are similar, they too should appear in similar form.

NO: She likes sun, the sand, and the sea.

YES: She likes the sun, the sand, and the sea.

NO: George is always singing, drumming, or he will play the guitar.

YES: George is always singing, drumming, or playing the guitar.

NO: Charlene's car skidded, turned sideways, then comes to a stop.

YES: Charlene's car skidded, turned sideways, and came to a stop.

Whenever *and* or *or* is used in a sentence, each must connect equal parts. Words are paired with words, phrases with phrases, clauses with clauses, and sentences with sentences. All these pairs must be *parallel;* they must have the same form.

NO: Her family went to London, to Amsterdam, and they even saw Rome and Paris!

YES: Her family went to London, to Amsterdam, and even to Rome and Paris!

NO: You can use this form to apply or if you want to change your status.

YES: You can use this form to apply or to change your status.

NO: Debby noticed the way Margie talked and how she kept looking at the desk.

YES: Debby noticed how Margie talked and how she kept looking at the desk.

Pairs of connectives, such as *both/and, either/or, neither/nor,* and *not only/ but also,* usually connect parallel structures.

NO: That book was both helpful and contained a lot of information.

YES: That book was both helpful and informative.

NO: So, my father said, "Either you come with us now, or stay here alone."

YES: So, my father said, "Either you come with us now, or you stay here alone."

NO: Here we either turn left or right, but I forget which.

YES: Here we turn either left or right, but I forget which.

NO: Karen bought the table both for beauty and utility.

YES: Karen bought the table for both beauty and utility.

Sentence Fragments

"Where did you go?"

"To the new movie theater. The one on Valley Street."

"Where on Valley Street?"

"Just past the train station, and across the street from the post office."

"See a good movie?"

"The best. Really funny, but serious, too."

"Sounds good."

Probably neither of the people in the conversation above realized that they were not using complete sentences. Only the first question, *"Where did you go?"* is a complete sentence. The rest are *sentence fragments.*

A sentence fragment is only a part of a sentence, because it is usually missing a subject or a verb.

NO:	So illogical!
YES:	It is so illogical!
NO:	Only for love, you see.
YES:	They did it only for love, you see.
NO:	No one. Not even the teacher.
YES:	No one, not even the teacher, could do it.

In conversation (as in the one above), there is a tendency to speak in sentence fragments, and so such fragments often appear in our writing. Proofreading and revision, however, can help to correct this error.

There are two ways to correct a sentence fragment. The first is to supply whatever is missing, as was done above. The other way is to attach the fragment to the sentence before or after it.

NO:	When I jog, especially in the early morning. I sometimes see the morning star.
YES:	When I jog, especially in the early morning, I sometimes see the morning star.
NO:	Because he was wrong. That's why he was embarrassed.
YES:	He was embarrassed because he was wrong.
NO:	Always and everywhere. She thought of him always and everywhere.
YES:	Always and everywhere, she thought of him.

It is not always incorrect to use sentence fragments. They are used to reproduce conversation and are also quite effective as questions and exclamations. Some examples are:

How absurd!

Now for some examples.

After all this? Not on your life!

The more we studied, the less we knew.

Although properly used sentence fragments can add spark, it is generally best to avoid using them except when more liveliness is needed.

Run-On Sentences

A run-on sentence contains two complete sentences totally fused.

NO:	It was a pleasant drive the sun was shining.
YES:	It was a pleasant drive because the sun was shining.
NO:	They are all similar materials they may not look or feel alike.
YES:	They are all similar materials, although they may not look or feel alike.
NO:	Susan said we passed the restaurant I think it's farther ahead.
YES:	Susan said we passed the restaurant. I think it's farther ahead.

Comma Splices

The run-on sentence is a very common error. Sometimes a writer will try to correct it by inserting a comma between the clauses, but this creates another error, a comma splice. The following examples illustrate various ways to correct the comma splice.

NO: Talk softly, someone is listening.

YES: Talk softly; someone is listening.

OR

Talk softly, because someone is listening.

NO: If you know, you must tell us, we will do it.

YES: If you know, you must tell us. Then we will do it.

NO: Take a hint from me, drive more slowly on this curve.

YES: Take a hint from me: drive more slowly on this curve.

NO: We were lost, the captain could not see the land.

YES: We were lost. The captain could not see the land.

Short, Choppy Sentences—Sentence Variation

Try to read the following passage:

There was a table set out under a tree. It was in front of the house. The March Hare and the Hatter were having tea at it. A Dormouse was sitting between them. He was fast asleep. The other two were using it as a cushion. They rested their elbows on it. They talked over its head. "Very uncomfortable for the Dormouse," thought Alice; "only, as it's asleep, I suppose it doesn't mind."

Notice how quickly you read when the sentences are short; you hardly have enough time to form a picture of the scene. It is as if the writer added each thought as it occurred to him, and in fact, this is usually the case. It is a sure sign of poor writing. Now read the same excerpt the way that Lewis Carroll wrote it.

> There was a table set out under a tree in front of the house, and the March Hare and the Hatter were having tea at it: a Dormouse was sitting between them, fast asleep, and the other two were using it as a cushion, resting their elbows on it and talking over its head. "Very uncomfortable for the Dormouse," thought Alice; "only, as it's asleep, I suppose it doesn't mind."

Sentence variation creates well-balanced, smooth writing that flows and gives the reader the feeling that the writer knows the subject. Although there is nothing grammatically wrong with short sentences, they often separate ideas that should be brought together.

NO: People change. Places change. Alan felt this. He had been away for ten years.

YES: On returning after a ten-year absence, Alan had a strong feeling of how people and places change.

NO: She looked at the sky. Then she looked at the sea. They were too big. She threw a rock in the ocean. She started to cry. Then she went home.

YES: The sky and the sea looked too big. She threw a rock into the ocean, and as it disappeared she began to cry. Then she turned to go home.

As a rule, avoid using chains of short, choppy sentences. Organize your thoughts and try to vary the length of your sentences.

Wordiness

Effective writing means concise writing. Wordiness, on the other hand, decreases clarity of expression by cluttering sentences with unnecessary words. Of course, short sentences are not necessarily better than long ones simply because they are brief. As long as a word serves a function, it should remain in the sentence. However, repetition of words, sounds, and phrases should be used only for emphasis or other stylistic reasons. Editing your writing will reduce its bulk. Notice the difference in impact between the first and second sentences in the following pairs.

NO: The medical exam that he gave me was entirely complete.

YES: The medical exam he gave me was complete.

NO: It seems perfectly clear to me that although he went and got permission from the professor, he still should not have played that awful, terrible joke on the dean.

YES: It seems clear to me that although he got permission from the professor, he still should not have played that terrible joke on the dean.

NO: It will be our aim to ensure proper health care for each and every one of the people in the United States.

YES: Our aim will be to ensure proper health care for all Americans.

Rambling Sentences

A rambling sentence continues on and on and seems to never end.

NO: The mountain was steep, but the road was clear; the sun was shining, and we all had the spirit of adventure in our heart and a song of the open road on our lips, so we took the turn that took our car up that steep mountain road.

YES: The mountain was steep, but the road was clear. The sun was shining. All of us had the spirit of adventure in our heart and a song of the open road on our lips. So we took our car up that steep mountain road.

There is often nothing grammatically wrong with a rambling sentence; it is simply too long, and it interferes with the reader's comprehension. Unfortunately, a writer who makes this kind of error tends to do it a lot. A good rule to follow is this: If a sentence runs for more than two typewritten lines, think twice about it. It should probably be recast.

III. WORDS COMMONLY CONFUSED AND MISUSED

The complex nature of language sometimes makes writing difficult. Words often become confusing when they have similar forms and sounds. Indeed, an author may have a correct meaning in mind, but an incorrect word choice can alter the meaning of a sentence or even make it totally illogical.

NO:	Martha was always part of that *cliché*.
YES:	Martha was always part of that *clique*.

(A *cliché* is a trite or hackneyed expression; a *clique* is an exclusive group of people.)

NO:	The minister spoke of the soul's *immorality*.
YES:	The minister spoke of the soul's *immortality*.

(*Immorality* means wickedness; *immortality* means imperishable or unending life.)

NO:	Where is the nearest *stationary* store?
YES:	Where is the nearest *stationery* store?

(*Stationary* means immovable; *stationery* is paper used for writing.)

Below are groups of words that are often confused because of their similar forms and sounds.

1. *a*   *A* is used before words beginning with a consonant sound.

   an   *An* is used before words with a vowel sound. This is an important distinction; it is not the spelling that determines whether to use *a* or *an*, but the sound.

                 an umbrella BUT a university

a radio   BUT an RCA record

an hour   BUT a human being

a historical event   BUT an honorary degree

2. **accent**   v. to stress or emphasize. (You must *accent* the last syllable.)

   ascent   n. a climb or rise. (John's *ascent* of the mountain was dangerous.)

   assent   n. consent, compliance. (We need your *assent* before we can go ahead with the plans.)

3. **accept**   v. to take something offered. (She *accepted* the gift.)

   except   prep. other than, but. (Everyone was included in the plans *except* him.)

4. **advice**   n. opinion given as to what to do or how to handle a situation. (Her sister gave her *advice* on what to say at the interview.)

   advise   v. to counsel. (John's guidance counselor *advised* him on which colleges to apply to.)

5. **affect**   v. to influence. (Mary's suggestion did not *affect* me.)

   effect   v. to cause to happen. (The plan was *effected* with great success.)   n. result. (The *effect* of the medicine is excellent.)

6. **allusion** — n. indirect reference. (In the poem, there are many biblical *allusions*.)

   illusion — n. false idea or conception; belief or opinion not in accord with the facts. (Greg was under the *illusion* that he could win the race after missing three weeks of practice.)

7. **already** — adv. previously. (I had *already* read that novel.)

   all ready — adv. + adj. prepared. (The family was *all ready* to leave on vacation.)

8. **altar** — n. table or stand used in religious rites. (The priest stood at the *altar*.)

   alter — v. to change. (Their plans were *altered* during the strike.)

9. **as if** — conj. as it would be if (It looks *as if* it's going to rain.)

   like — prep. inclined to (It looks *like* rain.)

10. **capital** — n. 1. a city where the government meets. (The senators had a meeting in Albany, the *capital* of New York.) 2. money used in business. (They had enough *capital* to develop the industry.)

   capitol — n. building in which the legislature meets. (Senator Brown gave a speech at the *Capitol* in Washington.)

11. **choose** — v. to select. (Which camera did you *choose*?)

   chose — past tense, choose. (Susan *chose* to stay home.)

12. cite   v. to quote. (The student *cited* evidence from the text.)

    site   n. location. (They chose the *site* where the house would be built.)

13. clothes   n. garments. (Because she got caught in the rain, her *clothes* were wet.)

    cloths   n. pieces of material. (The *cloths* were used to wash the windows.)

14. coarse   adj. rough, unrefined. (Sandpaper is *coarse*.)

    course   n. 1. path of action. (She did not know what *course* would solve the problem.)

     2. passage. (We took the long *course* to the lake.)

     3. series of studies. (We both enrolled in the physics *course*.)

     4. part of a meal. (She served a five-*course* meal.)

15. consul   n. a person appointed by the government to live in a foreign city and represent the citizenry and business interests of the native country there. (The *consul* was appointed to Naples, Italy.)

    council   n. a group used for discussion or advisement. (The *council* decided to accept his letter of resignation.)

    counsel   v. to advise. (Tom *counsels* Jerry on tax matters.)

16. **criterion**   n. (singular) standard (The only *criterion* is patience.)

     criteria   (plural) (There are several *criteria* applicants must meet.)

17. **decent**   adj. proper; respectable. (He was very *decent* about the entire matter.)

     descent   n. 1. moving down. (In Dante's *Inferno*, the *descent* into hell was depicted graphically.) 2. ancestry. (He is of Irish *descent*.)

18. **device**   n. 1. plan; scheme. (The *device* helped her win the race.) 2. invention. (We bought a *device* that opens the garage door automatically.)

     devise   v. to contrive. (He *devised* a plan so John could not win.)

19. **emigrate**   v. to go away from a country. (Many Japanese *emigrated* from Japan in the late 1800s.)

     immigrate   v. to come into a country. (Her relatives *immigrated* to the United States after World War I.)

20. **eminent**   n. prominent. (He is an *eminent* member of the community.)

     imminent   adj. impending. (The decision is *imminent*.)

     immanent   adj. existing within. (Maggie believed that religious spirit is *immanent* in human beings.)

21. **fair**   adj. 1. beautiful. (She was a *fair* maiden.)

     2. just. (She tried to be *fair*.)

n. festival. (There were many games at the *fair*.)

fare n. amount of money paid for transportation. (The city proposed that the subway *fare* be raised.)

22. farther adv. distance. (We travelled farther than we expected.)

further adv. furthermore; in depth. (We will discuss this *further*.)

23. forth adv. onward. (The soldiers moved *forth* in the blinding snow.)

fourth adj. 4th. (She was the *fourth* runner-up in the beauty contest.)

24. imply v. to suggest something. (I *implied* that I didn't approve of their actions.)

infer v. to drawer a conclusion from a remark or action. (I *inferred* from your letter that you will not be attending the meeting next week.)

25. insure v. to guarantee. (He *insured* his luggage before the flight.)

ensure v. to make certain. (*Ensure* your safety by driving carefully.)

26. its possessive form of *it*. (Our town must improve *its* roads.)

it's contraction of *it is*. (*It's* time to leave the party.)

27. later adj., adv. at a subsequent date. (We will take a vacation *later* this year.)

latter n. second of the two. (Susan can visit Monday or Tuesday. The *latter*, however, is preferable.)

28.	lead	n. a metal. (The handgun was made of *lead*.) v. to show the way. (The camp counselor *leads* the way to the picnic grounds.)
	led	past tense of verb *lead*. (The dog *led* the way.)
29.	lend	v. to let out for temporary use. (We are in the business of *lending* you money.)
	loan	n. money lent at interest. (The bank gave the student a *loan* for her tuition.)
30.	loose	adj. free, unrestricted. (The dog was let *loose* by accident.)
	lose	v. to suffer the loss of. (He was afraid he would *lose* the race.)
31.	moral	adj. virtuous. (She is a *moral* woman with high ethical standards.) n. lesson taught by a story, incident, etc. (Most fables end with a *moral*.)
	morale	n. mental condition. (After the team lost the game, their *morale* was low.)
32.	of	prep. from. (She is *of* French descent.)
	off	adv. away, at a distance. (The television fell *off* the table.)
33.	passed	past tense of verb *pass*. having satisfied some requirement. (He *passed* the test.)

	past	adj. gone by or elapsed in time. (His *past* deeds got him in trouble.) n. a period of time gone by. (His *past* was shady.) prep. beyond. (She ran *past* the house.)
34.	personal	adj. private. (Jack was unwilling to discuss his childhood; it was too *personal*.)
	personnel	n. staff. (The *personnel* at the department store was made up of young adults.)
35.	principal	n. head of a school. (The *principal* addressed the graduating class.) adj. main, most important. (JR was the *principal* character in the TV drama "Dallas.") or (The country's *principal* export is coffee.)
	principle	n. the ultimate source, origin, or cause of something; a law, truth. (The *principles* of physics were reviewed in class today.)
36.	prophecy	n. prediction of the future. (His *prophecy* that he would become a doctor came true.)
	prophesy	v. to declare or predict. (He *prophesied* that we would win the lottery.)
37.	quiet	adj. still; calm. (At night, all is *quiet*.)
	quite	adv. really, truly. (She is *quite* a good singer.)
	quit	v. to free oneself. (Peter had little time to spare, so he *quit* the chorus.)

38. respectfully — adv. with respect, honor, esteem. (He declined the offer *respectfully.*)

    respectively — adv. in the order mentioned. (Jack, Susan, and Jim, who are members of the club, were elected president, vice president, and secretary, *respectively.*)

39. stationary — adj. immovable. (The park bench is *stationary.*)

    stationery — n. paper used for writing. (The invitations were printed on yellow *stationery.*)

40. straight — adj. not curved. (The road was *straight.*)

    strait — adj. restricted, narrow, confined. (The patient was put into a *strait* jacket.) n. narrow waterway. (He sailed through the *Straits* of Magellan.)

41. than — conj. used most commonly in comparisons. (Maggie is older *than* I.)

    then — adv. soon afterward. (We lived in Boston; *then* we moved to New York.)

42. their — possessive form of *they.* (That is *their* house on Tenafly Drive.)

    they're — contraction of *they are. (They're* leaving for California next week.)

    there — adv. at that place. (Who is standing *there* under the tree?)

43. **to**   prep. in the direction of; toward. (She made a turn *to* the right onto Norman Street.)

     too   adv. 1. more than enough. (She served *too* much for dinner.) 2. also. (He is going to Maine *too*.)

     two   n. 2; the sum of one plus one. (We have *two* pet rabbits.)

44. **weather**   n. the general condition of the atmosphere. (The *weather* is expected to be clear on Sunday.)

     whether   conj. if it be a case or fact. (We don't know *whether* the trains are late.)

45. **who's**   contraction of *who is* or *who has*. (*Who's* willing to volunteer for the night shift?)

     whose   possessive form of *who*. (*Whose* book is this?)

46. **your**   possessive form of *you*. (Is this *your* seat?)

     you're   contraction of *you are*. (I know *you're* going to do well on the test.)

(sample appendix)

APPENDIX

When a Paper has Only One Source

If a term paper is written using only one source, a special way to make notes of sources is used. The first footnote in the text is the only true footnote. This footnote will give the author's name, the title of the book, the page of the reference, and all of the publication information. For all notes after this first footnote, all the writer needs to do is place the page reference in parenthesis in the text where the note is needed. Because of this system, no bibliography is needed.

For example, a term paper using only The Scarlet Letter by Nathaniel Hawthorne would need a solitary footnote, shown below. For all notes in the text that follow would have a structure such as: The soldiers were originally from the Niagara frontier (p. 23) but Roger Chillingworth lived in Oxford (p. 121).

If the term paper used a play for its only source, such as Shakespeare's Hamlet, then the notes after the first footnote would contain act, scene, and line references (I, ii, 23-30) instead of a page reference. An example would be: Hamlet makes reference to another of Shakespeare's classics Julius Caesar (III, ii, 109-110).

---

1. Nathaniel Hawthorne, The Scarlet Letter (New York: Barnes & Noble,Inc.,1993) 21.

(sample bibliography)

BIBLIOGRAPHY

Angelou, Maya. I Know Why the Caged Bird Sings. New York: Random House, 1969.

de la Croix, Horst et al. Art Through the Ages. Eighth edition, New York: Harcourt Brace Jovanovich, Publishers, vol. I, 1982.

Dible, Donald M., ed. What Everybody Should Know About Patents, Trademarks and Copyrights. Fairfield: The Entrepreneur Press, 1978.

Fitzgerald, Frances Scott. The Great Gatsby. New York: Charles Scribner's Sons, 1925.

Winchester, A.M. Modern Biology. Second edition, New York: Van Nostrand Reinhold Company, 1971.

Weinberg, Robert A. "Tumor Suppresser Genes." Science. American Association for the Advancement of Science, vol. 254, Nov. 22, 1991.

REA's
HANDBOOK OF
ENGLISH
Grammar, Style, and Writing

All the essentials you need to know are contained in this simple and practical book

Learn quickly and easily

- **Rules and exceptions in grammar**
- **Spelling and proper punctuation**
- **Common errors in sentence structure**
- **2,000 examples of correct usage**
- **Effective writing skills**

Complete practice exercises with answers follow each chapter

R͟E͟A *Research & Education Association*

Available at your local bookstore or order directly from us by sending in coupon below.

REA's Test Preps
The Best in Test Preparation

- REA "Test Preps" are **far more** comprehensive than any other test preparation series
- Each book contains up to **eight** full-length practice exams based on the most recent exams
- **Every** type of question likely to be given on the exams is included
- Answers are accompanied by **full** and **detailed** explanations

REA publishes more than 60 Test Preparation volumes in several series. They include:

Advanced Placement Exams (APs)
Biology
Calculus AB & Calculus BC
Chemistry
Computer Science
English Language & Composition
English Literature & Composition
European History
Government & Politics
Physics
Psychology
Statistics
Spanish Language
United States History

College-Level Examination Program (CLEP)
Analyzing and Interpreting Literature
College Algebra
Freshman College Composition
General Examinations
General Examinations Review
History of the United States I
Human Growth and Development
Introductory Sociology
Principles of Marketing
Spanish

SAT II: Subject Tests
American History
Biology
Chemistry
English Language Proficiency Test
French
German

SAT II: Subject Tests (cont'd)
Literature
Mathematics Level IC, IIC
Physics
Spanish
Writing

Graduate Record Exams (GREs)
Biology
Chemistry
Computer Science
Economics
Engineering
General
History
Literature in English
Mathematics
Physics
Political Science
Psychology
Sociology

ACT - ACT Assessment

ASVAB - Armed Services Vocational Aptitude Battery

CBEST - California Basic Educational Skills Test

CDL - Commercial Driver License Exam

CLAST - College Level Academic Skills Test

ELM - Entry Level Mathematics

ExCET - Exam for Certification of Educators in Texas

FE (EIT) - Fundamentals of Engineering Exam

FE Review - Fundamentals of Engineering Review

GED - High School Equivalency Diploma Exam (U.S. & Canadian editions)

GMAT - Graduate Management Admission Test

LSAT - Law School Admission Test

MAT - Miller Analogies Test

MCAT - Medical College Admission Test

MSAT - Multiple Subjects Assessment for Teachers

NJ HSPT- New Jersey High School Proficiency Test

PPST - Pre-Professional Skills Tests

PRAXIS II/NTE - Core Battery

PSAT - Preliminary Scholastic Assessment Test

SAT I - Reasoning Test

SAT I - Quick Study & Review

TASP - Texas Academic Skills Program

TOEFL - Test of English as a Foreign Language

TOEIC - Test of English for International Communication

RESEARCH & EDUCATION ASSOCIATION
61 Ethel Road W. • Piscataway, New Jersey 08854
Phone: (732) 819-8880

Please send me more information about your Test Prep books

Name _____

Address _____

City _____ State _____ Zip _____

MAXnotes®

REA's Literature Study Guides

MAXnotes® are student-friendly. They offer a fresh look at masterpieces of literature, presented in a lively and interesting fashion. **MAXnotes®** offer the essentials of what you should know about the work, including outlines, explanations and discussions of the plot, character lists, analyses, and historical context. **MAXnotes®** are designed to help you think independently about literary works by raising various issues and thought-provoking ideas and questions. Written by literary experts who currently teach the subject, **MAXnotes®** enhance your understanding and enjoyment of the work.

Available **MAXnotes®** include the following:

Absalom, Absalom!
The Aeneid of Virgil
Animal Farm
Antony and Cleopatra
As I Lay Dying
As You Like It
The Autobiography of
    Malcolm X
The Awakening
Beloved
Beowulf
Billy Budd
The Bluest Eye, A Novel
Brave New World
The Canterbury Tales
The Catcher in the Rye
The Color Purple
The Crucible
Death in Venice
Death of a Salesman
The Divine Comedy I: Inferno
Dubliners
The Edible Woman
Emma
Euripides' Medea & Electra
Frankenstein
Gone with the Wind
The Grapes of Wrath
Great Expectations
The Great Gatsby
Gulliver's Travels
Handmaid's Tale
Hamlet
Hard Times
Heart of Darkness

Henry IV, Part I
Henry V
The House on Mango Street
Huckleberry Finn
I Know Why the Caged
    Bird Sings
The Iliad
Invisible Man
Jane Eyre
Jazz
The Joy Luck Club
Jude the Obscure
Julius Caesar
King Lear
Leaves of Grass
Les Misérables
Lord of the Flies
Macbeth
The Merchant of Venice
Metamorphoses of Ovid
Metamorphosis
Middlemarch
A Midsummer Night's Dream
Moby-Dick
Moll Flanders
Mrs. Dalloway
Much Ado About Nothing
Mules and Men
My Antonia
Native Son
1984
The Odyssey
Oedipus Trilogy
Of Mice and Men
On the Road

Othello
Paradise
Paradise Lost
A Passage to India
Plato's Republic
Portrait of a Lady
A Portrait of the Artist
    as a Young Man
Pride and Prejudice
A Raisin in the Sun
Richard II
Romeo and Juliet
The Scarlet Letter
Sir Gawain and the
    Green Knight
Slaughterhouse-Five
Song of Solomon
The Sound and the Fury
The Stranger
Sula
The Sun Also Rises
A Tale of Two Cities
The Taming of the Shrew
Tar Baby
The Tempest
Tess of the D'Urbervilles
Their Eyes Were Watching God
Things Fall Apart
To Kill a Mockingbird
To the Lighthouse
Twelfth Night
Uncle Tom's Cabin
Waiting for Godot
Wuthering Heights
Guide to Literary Terms

RESEARCH & EDUCATION ASSOCIATION
61 Ethel Road W. • Piscataway, New Jersey 08854
Phone: (732) 819-8880

Please send me more information about MAXnotes®.

Name _____

Address _____

City _____ State _____ Zip _____

ST. B_____'S ACADEMY

0001 13645